ASSIMIL® on the Road

Produced by: **ASSIMIL France**

© Assimil, 1998   ISBN 2-7005-0245-X
This book is adapted from the German original **"Französisch
Wort für Wort"** (Reise Know-How Verlag Peter Rump GmbH,
Bielefeld, © Peter Rump).

French
From the Word GO!

Gabriele Kalmbach

adapted by David Applefield

Illustrated by J.-L. Goussé

B.P. 25
94431 Chennevières-sur-Marne Cedex
FRANCE

Assimil's On the Road Quick Recipe
for Speaking French and Being Understood!

Welcome! Here's the secret.

A small dose of French grammar. Just a hint. The simple stuff. Not all the rules. Nothing complicated to memorize. Just the basic rules, ready to plug-in and use as you need them. But enough of the structure and patterns of the language to enable you to create your own sentences quickly.

A healthy measure of conversation skills and realistic situations where you'll need and want to be able to participate and be understood. Seasoned with generous garnishings of translated words and easy-to-recognize phonetic spellings. Although we don't take sides, you'll note that we've used American-English spellings and expressions when faced with the choice. But, it's French that we care about first, so... **On y va !** (*oh-nee vah*)... Let's go!

Language is the key to participating in local life. You are a visitor, but you'd like to feel at home. You'll find here the beginning of that process. The index at the back gives you a down-and-dirty selection of words, although multiple usages and contexts are not indicated, so you have to try them out and watch facial expressions. Making mistakes is the only way to learn a foreign language. As the French are proud of their language and defend it all the time, they love when you – especially "Anglophones" – show a willingness to try.

With the essential ingredients compiled here, all that's missing is you – and your talent in pronouncing the words and sentences that you'll soon be ready to compose. Regarding the pronunciation, we've explained in the introduction the main points for getting you to create sounds that come out sounding like French. We reiterate here, the only pronunciation system worth its weight is one that works. We've spelled out words in a variety of manners with the sole intent of helping you to get your lips, tongue, mouth, nose, facial muscles, shoulders, etc. to play the right tune. But, like all instruments, you have to practice. So, get out "On the Road", stop into the cafés, stroll along the sidewalks, pull up to the dinner table, and start speaking **French From the Word GO!**

CONTENTS

INTRODUCTION

Welcome to French! In this compact book the emphasis is always on communicating, understanding, and being understood. Face it, that's what's important when you're in a foreign place as a visitor for a few days. Surviving, participating, enjoying. You don't have time to learn the language from the ground up; *au contraire* (that means "just the opposite"), you have to hit the ground running. You need a toilet. You want a good restaurant. Your hotel room is too noisy. You'd like to invite a French person to dinner. You have a flight to catch. Etc.

With regards to French grammar and all those confusing exceptions to complicated rules, we are comfortable simply guiding you through the very basics – all you need to get by in the beginning. And, as for the tenses, for starters let's just stick to the basic three: the past, present, and future. **Bon voyage** and **bon séjour** (that means "have a great stay")!

Where French is Spoken

French-speaking countries are more numerous than you might think. The *Francophonie* (French-speaking world) includes some 48 countries!

French is the mother tongue and official language of France, parts of Belgium and Switzerland, Luxembourg, Monaco, Andorra, St. Pierre and Miquelon, Guadeloupe, Martinique, French Guyana, the Reunion Island, Mayotte, Vanuatu, New Caledonia, French Polynesia, Wallis and Futuna, and of course Quebec.

In addition, French is the official language – and the language of instruction in schools – in much of Africa, including Benin, Burkina Faso, Burundi, Comores, Djibuti, Ivory Coast, Gabon, Guinea, Cameroun, Congo, Madagascar, Mauritania, Niger, Rwanda, Senegal, Seychelles Islands, Chad, Togo, and Central African Republic.

French is the vehicular language as well in Algeria, Morocco, Tunisia, Lebanon, Cambodia, Vietnam, Laos, Mauritius, and is widely used due to its former status as a colonial language.

In several regions, French is officially recognized as a local language. Such is the case in Jersey in the Channel Islands, the Valley of Aoste in northern Italy, the US State of Louisiana and the Indian city of Pondichery. Of course each of these regions or cities hosts its own dialect rich in local vocabulary, pronunciation and usage. But it's all French.

It's useful to know that in France a "centralization" of the language dates back to the 17th century when a concentrated effort to unify the French language began. This occurred both in the spoken language (to the detriment of regional languages and local dialects) and in the written language. Only over the last few decades has there been a wave of regional movements keen on decentralizing cultural dominance and regaining for their local languages the position and prominence that they once maintained. The principal languages concerned include: Occitan, Provençal, Breton, Basque, Alsatian, and Corsican. Whatever the case, it will be French though that you'll be using to communicate in France and its constellations of lands within its linguisitic influence.

Pronunciation and Intonation

French unfortunately is not exactly pronounced like it is written! Certain letters take on different pronunciations whether they precede or follow another letter. But, once you learn a few simple rules, these variations should not pose too many problems for you.

Pronunciation and Phonetic Transcription

In that you can hardly assimilate everything at once, we offer here phonetic transcriptions as well, which you'll find useful throughout **French From the Word GO!** To start with, here is a quick guide for pronouncing the letters in the French alphabet, useful when spelling your name, for example, over the phone.

a = ah	h = ahsh	o = oh	v = vay
b = bay	i = ee	p = pay	w = doobleh vay
c = say	j = jzee	q = kew	x = eeks
d = day	k = kah	r = air	y = eegrek
e = uh	l = el	s = es	z = zed
f = ehf	m = em	t = tay	
g = jzay	n = en	u = ew	

Pronunciation Guide

It would be too long and difficult to attempt to provide here all the details concerning French pronunciation. So, instead of including a strict and systematic phonetic transcription, we decided to transcribe the French words in the simplest, most direct way so that when you read them out loud (as if the words were in English) you'll end up sounding like you speak French! **Don't worry if you find inconsistencies in the way we've transcribed French words**. We've taken into account the context of words in a sentence, and all that matters is that you start pronouncing sounds that are understood as French. **The key is to just read the transcription as if it were English**.

Having said that, here are a few remarks concerning special, and specifically difficult sounds in French.
• **h** in French is silent. Example: hospital is **hôpital** (*ohpeetal*).
• **s, t, d, e** in French are silent when they land at the end of a word. Examples: **voitures** (*vwatur*), **ils mangent** (*eel ma-njze*), **moutarde** (*mootard*).

3

• Certain sounds in French don't exist in English. The sound "u" for example, which in French sounds like the grunt you'd make if someone were to hit you in the stomach! Other sounds are close to the English but not exactly the same. We've transcribed them as close as we can to help you sound as French as possible.

• The letters e, é, è/ê are all pronounced differently. The best way to learn them is by example. Note: **e** without an accent is always pronounced like the e in merchant: **chemise** (*shemeez*). Compare: **é** (called "*e accent aigu*") comes close to the **e** in the word h**a**y or the **a** in the word M**a**y with the corners of your lips stretching toward your ears.

When the accent goes the other way, **è**, ("*e accent grave*") or there is a ^ ("*accent circonflexe*") over the **e**, the sound is like the e in h**a**y or the **a** in M**a**y but with your mouth more open.

Stress

In French, generally, it's the last syllable in a word that is stressed. For example, in bon**jour**, **"jour"** is pronounced with slightly more stress and longer than **"bon."** It's the same with mer**ci** where **"ci"** is pronounced with greater insistence than **"mer."** In the phonetic transcriptions the stressed syllables have been <u>underlined</u> for your convenience.

Nasal Sound

These sounds are hard to explain and not easy to create. We've indicated these sounds with a hyphen before the **n** or **m**. You'll encounter often the following "nasal" sounds in many French words. By nasal, we mean that the sound seems to resonate at the back of your throat and in your nasal cavity. One way of reproducing this sound is to try sending the sound up into your nostrils. Create this very French speech characteristic by pinching your nose when you say words like bread, **pain**. Say *pa-n*. Try **maman**, the word for mom. Say *mahmo-n*. Remember, the nasal *n/m* is barely pronounced.

Here are the letters in French words that are pronounced in this nasal fashion:

an, am, **en, em**	pronounce like your nose is stuffed up and then hardly pronounce the n	**enfant** *o-nfo-n* **embrasse** *o-mbrahss*
ain, aim, **in, im,** **ein, eim,** **un, ym**	pronounce like the dentist is holding down your tongue	**main** *ma-n*, **vin** *va-n*, **timbre** *ta-mbr*, **Reims** *ra-nss*, **un** *a-n*
oin **on, om**		**besoin** *bezwa-n* **montagne** *moh-ntahnye*

Liaisons

A *liaison* in spoken French is simply the sound that joins the letters of two distinct words, a practice which is common in the French language. This occurs when a word finishes with a consonant or a silent e and the following word begins with a vowel. The two words are thus read like one word. Example: her friend is **son ami** *sso-nami*. In the liaison the final consonant, even when it is silent, keeps its sound. Example: **les amis** (*layzamee*). Careful though, the letter d in a liaison is pronounced like a t. Example: **grand ami** (*gro-ntamee*). Similarly, the **s** and **x** are pronounced like a **z**.

5

Example: **deux amis** (*duhzamee*). We're almost finished. With the ending letters **rd** and **rt**, the liaison is between the **r** and the next word. In other words, don't pronounce the **d** or **t**. Example: **regard amusé** *(regar amoozay)*. Finally, the liaison does not apply to the word **et**, meaning "and".

Exercise in Pronunciation

Here, accompanied with their phonetic transcriptions, are the most common forms of greetings in French. Practice saying them out loud in that you'll certainly be using them often.

Bonjour
boh-nzoor
Hello /Good day.

Bonne nuit
bunnwee
Good night.

Bonsoir
boh-nswar
Good afternoon.

Au revoir
ohrevwar
Goodbye.

Salut
saloo
Hi.

À bientôt
ahbeeyentoh
See you soon.

S'il vous plaît (= SVP)
seelvooplay
Please.

Merci
mairsee
Thank you.

Ça va ?
sah vah?
How's it going?

A Few Common Word Helpers

Before taking on the Grammar Section, let's slow down for a second to consider a few word combinations which are both easy to grasp and very useful. They'll come in handy right away in lots of real life situations.

Il y a *illeeyah*   there is / there are

Simply translated as *there are* or *there is*, **il y a** will be at the front of hundreds of your statements in everyday French. And to create a question that begins with: Is there...? or Are there...? you repeat the same structure **Il y a**. Simply raise your voice at the end of the sentence to indicate that your question is in fact a question:

Il y a un taxi / un médecin ?   **Il y a des magasins ?**
illeeyah a-n taxi / a-n medsa-n ?   *illeeyah day magasa-n ?*
Is there a taxi /a doctor?   Are there stores?

Il y a de la place dans le taxi ?
illeeyah duh la plas daah-n luh taxi ?
He's there room in the taxi?

Oui, (il y a un taxi) / (il y a un médecin).
wee (illeeyah a-n taxi) / (illeeyah a-n medsa-n)
Yes, there is a taxi / there is a doctor.

Note the negative construction for *there is not / there are not*: simply add an **n'** before the **y** and **pas** after the **a**.

Non, (il n'y a pas de taxi / il n'y a pas de médecin).
noh-n, illneeyah pah duh taxi / illneeyah pah duh medsa-n
No, there isn't a taxi/there isn't a doctor.
or
Non, il n'y a en a pas.
no-hn, illneeyo-napah
No, there isn't.

You can of course vary your response depending on the type of information you're being asked for. Here are some other possible questions:

IL Y A DE LA PLACE DANS LE TAXI ?

Où est... ?   *Oow ay ?*   Where is...?

Où est la route vers Lille ?
Oow ay lah root vair <u>Leel</u> ?
Where's the road to Lille?

Où est le cinéma ?
Oow ay luh sinay<u>mah</u> ?
Where's the cinema/movie house?

Où est l'arrêt du bus ?
Oow ay lar<u>ray</u> doo <u>booss</u> ?
Where is the bus stop?

Qu'est-ce que... ?   *Keskuh... ?*   What is...?

You know already how to pose a certain number of questions.
Now here are two that we recommend you learn by heart from the
phonetic transcription. Don't forget to accentuate the last syllable
of every question!

Qu'est-ce que c'est ?   **Qu'est-ce qu'il y a ?**
Keskuh <u>say</u> ?   *<u>Keskilleeyah</u> ?*
What is this?   What's the matter?

GRAMMAR

Let the Grammar Begin!

French grammar as presented here should serve to help you
understand how the language functions.
We have provided the essentials and basic models needed for
constructing simple sentences and from which you can then go
further when you're ready to build more complex structures.
Remember, it's not important to keep in mind all the rules,
exceptions and nuances at once. Just be able to use what you need,
when you need it, without much effort.

Nouns

Gender

In French, unlike in English, nouns are either masculine or
feminine. There is no neuter gender. It is highly advisable to learn
each word with the article. You may wonder how French people
remember each time if it's **le** or **la**. Well, they don't. From early
childhood they learned that the word for dog is **le chien**, not simply
chien. So, learn the article with the noun. And be careful, what
seems like it should be masculine (or feminine) often isn't.

9

le garçon	*luh garsoh-n*	boy
la fille	*lah fee*	girl
le livre	*luh leevr*	book
la chemise	*la shemeez*	shirt

Common Feminine Word Endings

When you see these at the end of a noun you can assume the word is feminine.

-tié	l'amitié	*lahmeeteeyeh*	friendship
-tion	l'attention	*lato-nseeyoh-n*	attention
-erie	la boulangerie	*lah boolo-njzuhree*	bakery
-té	la nationalité	*lah nasseeyohnahleetay*	nationality
-ence	l'essence	*lesso-ns*	gasoline
-esse	la sagesse	*las sahjzess*	wisdom
-ise	la bêtise	*lah beteez*	foolishness

Common Masculine Word Endings

When you see these at the end of a noun you can assume the word is masculine

-on	le garçon	*luh garsoh-n*	boy
-age	le voyage	*luh vwayajz*	trip
-eau	le bateau	*luh bahto*	boat
-ail	le travail	*luh travaii*	work
-ment	le monument	*luh monoomo-n*	monument

Note as well that the days of the week, the months of the year, the seasons and directions are all masculine.

Plural Forms

In most cases, you simply add an s to nouns to create the plural form. But, this s is not pronounced.

le café	*luh cafay*	**les cafés**	*lay cafay*
la baguette	*lah baguet*	**les baguettes**	*lay baguet*

Articles

Definite Articles

In French, as you already know, there are two definite articles in the singular: **la** (feminine) and **le** (masculine).

la maison	*lah mayzoh-n*	house
le jardin	*luh jzarda-n*	garden

le (*luh*) (masculine)

le copain	*luh copa-n*	friend, pal
le garçon	*luh garsoh-n*	boy
le vélo	*luh vaylo*	bike

la (*lah*) (feminine)

la copine	*lah kopeen*	friend
la femme	*lah fahm*	wife
la voiture	*lah vwatur*	car

When they precede a word that begins with a vowel, both **le** and **la** become **l'**:

l'homme	*lumm*	man
l'argent	*larjzo-n*	money

11

In plural nouns, whether masculine or feminine, the article becomes **les** (*le*):

les hommes	*layzohm*	men
les femmes	*lay fahm*	women
les enfants	*layzo-nfo-n*	children

As usual in French, though, there are exceptions. Some nouns – those that end with **-eau** for example – take an **x** when plural.

le bateau	*luh bahto*	the boat
les bateaux	*lay bahto*	boats

Indefinite Articles

Here too, there are two articles in the singular form: **une** (feminine) and **un** (masculine):

The plural form for the two genders is **des.**

des vélos	*day vaylo*	bikes
des ordinateurs	*dayzordeenatuhr*	computers

Partitive Articles

These are a bit more tricky for English speakers. When a noun is preceded by the French word for of, **de**, the definite article in the masculine form changes. It's easy to remember when you see it. If you don't master this variation right away, don't fret. No one is going to judge you. The important thing is to understand and be understood:

masculine	**de le**	becomes	**du**	*doo*
feminine	**de la**	remains	**de la**	*duh lah*
l'	**de l'**	remains	**de l'**	*duhl*
pl.	**de les**	becomes	**des**	*day*

12

LES BATEAUX

A few examples:

de l'eau	*duhloh*	water
du vin	*doo va-n*	wine
du pain	*doo pa-n*	bread
du vent	*doo vo-n*	wind
du brouillard	*doo brueeare*	fog

Je **veux** is *I want* and **je voudrais** is *I would like*. Here's a quick review of the indefinite articles with **veux** and **voudrais**:

Je voudrais du café.
Jze voodray doo cafay.
I would like coffee.

Je veux de la confiture.
Jze voodray duh lah coh-nfeetur.
I want (some) jam.

JE VOUDRAIS UN CAFÉ.

Tu veux du thé ou du café ?
Too vuh doo <u>tay</u> oow doo ca<u>fay</u> ?
Do you want tea or coffee?

Pronouns

Personal Pronouns

One of the great differences between French and English and one of the most confusing cultural and linguistic barriers is the use in French of **tu** and **vous** as forms of **you**. **Tu** is familiar and **vous** is formal, but as an English speaker your idea of when it's okay to be familiar probably doesn't coincide with what's right in a French context. Remember, it's much better to err on the formal side than on the familiar. Use **vous** until the French person clearly invites you to **tutoyer** him or her – and don't switch over until that happens. And, it may not!

Table of Pronouns:

I	**je** *jze*	**me** *muh*	**me** *muh*
you	**tu** *too*	**te** *tuh*	**te** *tuh*
he	**il** *ill*	**lui** *lwee*	**le** *luh*
she	**elle** *el*	**lui** *lwee*	**la** *lah*
we	**nous** *noo*	**nous** *noo*	**nous** *noo*
you	**vous** *voo*	**vous** *voo*	**vous** *voo*
they (m)	**ils** *ill*	**leur** *luhr*	**les** *lay*
they (f)	**elles** *el*	**leur** *luhr*	**les** *lay*

Note that **je** becomes **j'**, **le** and **la** become **l'** and **tu** becomes **t'** when they precede a word that begins with a vowel.

J'ai une maison.
Jzay oon mayzoh-n
I have a house.

Je t'aime.
Jze tem.
I love you.

Indefinite Pronouns

In spoken French you'll hear very often **nous** (we) replaced by **on** (one).

On va au cinéma.
Oh-n vah owe seenay<u>ma</u>.
We're going to the cinema.

Possessive Pronouns

	Masculine	Feminine	Plural
my	**mon** *moh-n*	**ma** *mah*	**mes** *may*
your	**ton** *toh-n*	**ta** *tah*	**tes** *tay*
his/her	**son** *soh-n*	**sa** *sah*	**ses** *say*
our	**notre** *nohtr*	**notre** *nohtr*	**nos** *noh*
your	**votre** *vohtr*	**votre** *vohtr*	**vos** *voh*
their	**leur** *luhr*	**leur** *luhr*	**leurs** *luhr*

15

Remember that the possessive pronoun takes the gender of the object being possessed, not that of the one who possesses. **Son livre** can be either **à elle** (hers) or **à lui** (his).

C'est mon vélo.
Say moh-n vaylo.
It's my bike.

Ce sont ses enfants.
Suh soh-n sayzo-nfo-n.
They are his/her children.

Ce sont nos valises.
Suh soh-n no valeez.
They're our suitcases.

Anne est ma sœur.
Ahnnai mah suhr.
Anne is my sister.

Demonstrative Pronouns

This / These

masculine **this**	ce	*suh*
	cet	*set*
feminine **this**	cette	*set*
plural **these**	ces	*say*

The pronoun form depends on the gender and person of the noun.

ce vélo	*suh vaylo*	this bike
cet ordinateur	*set ordeenatuhr*	this computer
cette voiture	*set vwuatur*	this car
ces pommes	*say pum*	these apples

Pronouns that Reinforce

In French, unlike in English, when the speaker wants to emphasize that it is he or she that is speaking, the pronoun form is repeated:

Moi, je suis le premier.
Mwa jze swee luh pruhmeeyeh.
Me, I'm the first.

or

J'aime ça, moi.
Jzem sah, mwa.
I like that, me.

On the telephone one says:

Allo, c'est toi ?
Alloh, say twa ?
Hello, is that you?

Oui, c'est moi.
Wee, say mwa.
Yes, it's me.

These pronouns also serve to emphasize the possessor:

Ce livre est à moi !
Suh leevr etta mwa.
This book is **mine.**

This first form emphasizes the act of possession more than the second.

Adjectives

Adjectives in French change endings depending on the gender of the noun and whether the noun is singular or plural. This causes English speakers a lot of problems. Again, don't panic. Even if you miss-match your adjective forms, you'll be understood.

Note:
•In the Index at the back of this book, adjectives are generally listed in their masculine form.
•To create a feminine ending all you have to do is add an **e** to the masculine.
•To form a plural you almost always add an **s** to both the masculine and the feminine.

17

Singular	Plural
le grand bâtiment	**les grands bâtiments**
luh gro-n bahteemo-n	*lay gro-n bahteemo-n*
the big building	the big buildings
la grande ville	**les grandes villes**
lah gro-nd veel	*lay gro-nd veel*
the big city	the big cities
un grand appartement	**de grands appartements**
a-n gro-ntahpartuhmo-n	*duh gro-nzahpartuhmo-n*
a large apartment	large apartments

Remember – certain letters are silent! Don't forget to read carefully the phonetic transcriptions.

UN GRAND BÂTIMENT

18

Qualifying adjectives are placed *either* before or after the noun. There are a number of rules here, but we prefer not to confuse you with too many details. Keep going!

Note that the plural article **des** becomes **de** when it is placed directly before the adjective:

des appartements
dayzahpartuhmo-n
apartments

de grands appartements
duh gro-nzahpartuhmo-n
big apartments

l'économie française
layconomee fro-nsez
the French economy

la pomme verte
lah pum vairt
the green apple

le parti Socialiste
luh partee sosseeyahlist
the Socialist party

As we've already mentioned, the feminine form of adjectives is generally created by adding an **e** to the masculine ending. However, there are exceptions! Here is a list of commonly used adjectives in the masculine, the feminine and then their opposites.

beau / belle
boh / bel
beautiful / handsome

laid / laide
lay / led
ugly

bon / bonne
boh-n / bun
good

mauvais / mauvaise
mohvay / mohvez
bad

long / longue
loh-n / loh-ng
long

court / courte
coor / coort
short

lent / lente
lo-n / lo-nt
slow

rapide / rapide
*rah_peed_ / rah_peed_*
fast, quick

ouvert / ouverte
oovair / oovairt
open

fermé / fermée
*fair_may_ / fair_may_*
closed

jeune / jeune
jzun / jzun
young

vieux / vieille
*vee_yuh_ / vee_yey_*
old

plein / pleine
pla-n / plen
full

vide / vide
veed / veed
empty

cher / chère
shair / shair
dear, expensive

bon marché / bon marché
boh-n mar_shay_ / ...
cheap

bas / basse
bah / bass
low

haut / haute
oh / oht
high

facile / facile
*fas_seel_ / fas_seel_*
easy

difficile / difficile
deefees_seel_ / ...
difficult

juste / juste
jzoost / jzoost
true

faux / fausse
foh / foss
false, fake

froid / froide
frxwah / frwahd
cold

chaud / chaude
shoh / shohd
hot

léger / légère
layjzay / layjzair
light

lourd / lourde
loor / loord
heavy

It's easy in French to make sentences using adjectives.

20

Le vélo est rapide.		**Le ciel est bleu.**
Luh vaylo ay rah<u>peed</u>.		*Luh seeyell ay <u>bluh</u>.*
The bike is fast.		The sky is blue.

Here are the colors in French:

bleu / bleue	*bluh / ...*	blue
rose / rose	*rose / ...*	pink
blanc / blanche	*blo-n / blo-nsh*	white
marron / marron	*mah<u>roh-n</u> / ...*	brown
noir / noire	*nwar / ...*	black
jaune / jaune	*jzohn / ...*	yellow
vert / verte	*vair / vairt*	green
violet / violette	*veeyo<u>lay</u> / veeyo<u>lett</u>*	purple
rouge / rouge	*roojz / ...*	red
orange / orange	*oh<u>ro-nzj</u> / ...*	orange

Comparative and Superlative Forms

Comparatives are formed by placing the words **plus** (more) or **moins** (less) in front of the adjective:

plus cher	**moins cher**
ploo shair	*mwa-n shair*
more expensive	less expensive

plus ancien	**moins ancien**
ploozo-nsee<u>ye-n</u>	*mwa-nzo-nsee<u>ye-n</u>*
older	younger

Superlatives are formed with **le/la plus** (the most) or **le/la moins** (the least) and **les plus/les moins** for the plural.

bon	*boh-n*	good
meilleur	*may<u>yuhr</u>*	better
le meilleur	*luh may<u>yuhr</u>*	the best

mauvais	*mohvay*	bad
pire	*peer*	worse
le pire	*luh peer*	the worst
jeune	*jzun*	young
plus jeune	*ploo jzun*	younger
le plus jeune	*luh ploo jzun*	the youngest (masc.)
la plus jeune	**lah ploo jzun**	the youngest (fem.)
les plus jeunes	*lay ploo jzun*	the youngest (plural)

Some examples:

Il a le vélo le plus rapide.
Illah luh vaylo luh ploo rahpeed.
He has the fastest bike.

Il est le plus gentil.
Illay luh ploo jzo-ntee.
He is the nicest (one).

Elle est la plus intelligente.
Elay lah plooza-ntelleejzo-nt.
She is the most intelligent.

Ils sont les plus petits.
Illsoh-n lay ploo pehtee.
They are the smallest.

Comparisons

To make a comparison, simply add the little word: **que**. When the **que** comes before a word beginning with a vowel, replace the **e** with a '.

La voiture est plus rapide que le vélo.
Lah vwatur eh ploo rahpeed kuh luh vaylo.
The car is faster than the bike.

Aller à pied est moins rapide qu'aller en vélo.
Allay ah pyay eh mwa-n rahpeed kallay o-n vaylo.
Going by foot is slower than going by bike.

You can also compare two things of equal value by using **aussi... que**.

Julie est aussi grande que Céline.
Jzoolee etohsee gro-nd kuh Sayleen.
Julie is as tall as Céline.

Adverbs

Most adverbs, in French as in English, are easy to recognize.

Regular adverbs in French are generally formed by simply adding the ending **-ment** to the feminine form of the adjective.

Adjective Feminine		Adverb		
lente	*lo-nt*	**lentement**	*lo-ntuhmo-n*	slowly
rapide	*rahpeed*	**rapidement**	*rahpeeduhmo-n*	rapidly
heureuse	*erruhz*	**heureusement**	*erruhzuhmo-n*	luckily

Remember, adverbs are **always** placed behind the verb.

to run fast	**courir rapidement**	*cooreer rahpeeduhmo-n*
to eat late	**manger tard**	*mo-jzay tahr*

There are some irregular forms, too. Fortunately, there aren't many, but the most common ones are worth your taking the time to learn.

Adjective		Adverb		
bon	*boh-n*	**bien**	*beeye-n*	good
mauvais	*mohvay*	**mal**	*mahl*	bad
peu de	*puh duh*	**peu**	*puh*	little
beaucoup de	*bohkoo duh*	**beaucoup**	*bohkoo*	a lot

Il y a un bon film ce soir.
Illeeyah a-n boh-n film suh swar.
There is a good film tonight.

Le film raconte bien l'histoire.
Luh film racoh-nt beeye-n leestwar.
The film tells the story well .

Conjunctions

et	*ay*	and
mais	*may*	but
donc	*doh-nk*	thus
ou	*oow*	or
aussi	*ohsee*	also
comme	*cum*	how
si	*see*	if, when, as
parce que	*parskuh*	because
que	*kuh*	such as, that

Word Order in Simple Sentences

The simplest form is: subject–verb–object.

Je	**suis**	**Française.**
Jze	*swee*	*fro-nsez.*
I	am	French (woman).

24

Tu	as	**un vélo.**
Too	*ah*	*a-n vay<u>lo</u>.*
You	have	a bike.

But watch out! When the object is a personal pronoun it comes before the verb.

J'aime Nathalie.	**Je t'aime.**
Jzem Natah<u>lee</u>.	*Jze tem.*
I love Nathalie.	I love you.

Auxiliaries / Helping Verbs

Let's look at the two most important verbs in French: **être** (to be) and **avoir** (to have). No need to panic, but they are highly irregular and so you simply must learn how to use them.

Être

être	*etr*	to be
je suis	*jze <u>swee</u>*	I am
tu es	*too <u>eh</u>*	you are
il est	*ill <u>eh</u>*	he is
elle est	*el <u>eh</u>*	she is
nous sommes	*noo <u>sum</u>*	we are
vous êtes	*voo<u>zet</u>*	you are
ils sont	*ill<u>soh-n</u>*	they are (m)
elles sont	*el<u>soh-n</u>*	they are (f)

Je suis étudiante.	**Nous sommes ensemble.**
jze swee etud<u>io-nt</u>.	*Noo sum o-n<u>so-m</u>bl.*
I am a student.	We are together.

Tu es Tunisien.	**Vous êtes jeunes.**
Too eh Tuneesee<u>ye-n</u>.	*Voozet <u>jzun</u>.*
You are Tunisien.	You are young.

25

La fille est sympa.
Lah fee eh sa-npa.
The girl is nice.

Ils sont trop chers.
Illsoh-n troh shair.
They are too expensive.

Avoir

avoir	*avwar*	to have
j'ai	*jzay*	I have
tu as	*too ah*	you have
il a	*illah*	he has
elle a	*elah*	she has
nous avons	*noozavoh-n*	we have
vous avez	*voozavay*	you have
ils ont	*illzoh-n*	they have (m)
elles ont	*elzoh-n*	they have (f)

J'ai raison.
jzay rayzoh-n
I'm right.

Nous avons soif.
Noozavoh-n swaf.
We are thirsty.

Elle a froid.
Elah fwa.
She's cold.

Ils ont faim.
Illzoh-n fa-n.
They are hungry.

Expressions Using Avoir

avoir

avoir honte	*avwar oh-nt*	to be ashamed
avoir pitié	*avwar peeteeyay*	to pity
avoir faim	*avwar fa-n*	to be hungry
avoir horreur de	*avwar orruhr duh*	to be horrified by
avoir froid	*avwar frwa*	to be cold
avoir envie de	*avwar o-nvee*	to desire
en avoir marre	*o-n avwar mahr*	to be fed up
avoir peur	*avwar puhr*	to be afraid

avoir raison	*avwar raysoh-n*	to be right
avoir besoin	*avwar buhswa-n*	to need
être branché *(Slang)*	*etr bro-nshay*	to be tuned in
être en train de	*etr o-n tra-n duh*	to be in the process of
être à sec *(Slang)*	*etrahssek*	to be broke

Conjugating Verbs

In French, there are three groups of regular verbs, all easy to recognize by their endings:

> 1. Verbs that end in **-er**
> 2. Verbs that end in **-ir**
> 3. Verbs that end in **-re**

And of course there are the irregular verbs too! But it makes little sense at this point to tire you out with too many of these. You won't be able to learn them all at once. Even if you use a wrong form you'll be understood. We advise that you start by learning the infinitives and first person singular form.

With that you'll already be able to say lots of things. Almost all dictionaries include lists of the irregular verbs. If need be, check one out.

Tenses

Verbs in the present tense

-er verbs	**parler** *(parlay)*	to speak
je	**parle**	*parl*
tu	**parles**	*parl*
il / elle / on	**parle**	*parl*
nous	**parlons**	*parloh-n*
vous	**parlez**	*parlay*
ils / elles	**parlent**	*parl*

It's easier to speak French than to write it. For example, the first three persons in the singular are pronounced identically while they are written differently. A large number of verbs belong to this first group of **-er** verbs. A few prime examples: **manger** (to eat), **donner** (to give), **montrer** (to show), **aimer** (to love), **demander** (to ask), **rencontrer** (to meet), **écouter** (to listen), etc.

-ir verbs	**partir** (*parteer*)	to leave
je	**pars**	*par*
tu	**pars**	*par*
il / elle / on	**part**	*par*
nous	**partons**	*part<u>oh-n</u>*
vous	**partez**	*part<u>ay</u>*
ils / elles	**partent**	*part*

The verbs **finir** (to finish), **dormir** (to sleep), **courir** (to run), **sentir** (to smell, to feel), among others, are conjugated according to this model.

Attention! Verbs that end in **-oir**, like **savoir** (to know), **pouvoir** (to be able), **vouloir** (to want), and **devoir** (must), don't belong in this category. (See below the conjugations of **vouloir** and **pouvoir** and use them as guides.)

-re verbs	**comprendre** (*coh-mpro-ndr*)	understand
je	**comprends**	*coh-m<u>pro-n</u>*
tu	**comprends**	*coh-m<u>pro-n</u>*
il / elle / on	**comprend**	*coh-m<u>pro-n</u>*
nous	**comprenons**	*coh-mpre<u>noh-n</u>*
vous	**comprenez**	*coh-mpre<u>nay</u>*
ils / elles	**comprennent**	*coh-mpre<u>nn</u>*

Prendre (to take) is conjugated as well in this way. But watch out, **faire** (to do, to make), **boire** (to drink), **dire** (to say, to tell), and **croire** (to believe), are irregulars and don't follow this model.

The following highly irregular French verbs are extremely important. Learn them!

aller (to go)

je	vais	*vay*
tu	vas	*va*
il	va	*va*
nous	allons	*aloh-n*
vous	allez	*alay*
ils	vont	*voh-n*

faire (to make, do)

je	fais	*fay*
tu	fais	*fay*
il	fait	*fay*
nous	faisons	*fezoh-n*
vous	faites	*fett*
ils	font	*foh-n*

vouloir (to want)

je	veux	*vuh*
tu	veux	*vuh*
il	veut	*vuh*
nous	voulons	*vooloh-n*
vous	voulez	*voolay*
ils	veulent	*vuhll*

pouvoir (to be able, can)

je	peux	*puh*
tu	peux	*puh*
il	peut	*puh*
nous	pouvons	*poovoh-n*
vous	pouvez	*poovay*
ils	peuvent	*puhv*

Expressions using the verb "**faire**"

faire confiance   to have confidence in, to trust
Je te fais confiance avec ma voiture.
Jze tuh fay coh-nfeeyo-ns ahvek mah vwatur.
I trust you with my car.

faire du stop   to hitchhike
On a fait du stop jusqu'à Chicago.
Oh-nah fay doo stup jzooskah Sheecahgo.
We hitchhiked to Chicago.

faire la cuisine   to cook, to prepare a meal
Je fais la cuisine tous les vendredis soir.
Jze fay lah kweeizeen too lay vo-ndredee swar.
I cook every Friday night.

29

faire la gueule (slang) to pout, to "bitch"
> **Il fait la gueule depuis notre dispute.**
> *Ill fay lah gull duhpwee nohtr dispewt.*
> He's been pouting since our fight.

faire la lessive to do the laundry
> **Jacques refuse de faire la lessive.**
> *Jzak ruhfooz duh fair lah lesseev.*
> Jacques refuses to do the laundry.

faire la queue to wait in line
> **Nous faisons la queue depuis un quart d'heure.**
> *Noo fezoh-n la kuh duhpwee a-n kahr duhr.*
> We've been waiting in line for fifteen minutes.

faire la vaisselle to wash the dishes
> **Marcel et Claudine font la vaisselle ensemble.**
> *Marsel eh Clohdeen foh-n lah vessel o-nso-mbl.*
> Marcel and Claudine wash the dishes together.

faire le plein to fill up
> **Faire le plein de ma Peugeot coûte 300 francs.**
> *Fair luh pla-n duh mah Puhjzoh coot trwa so-n fro-n.*
> It costs me 300 francs to fill up my Peugeot.

il fait chaud / froid it's hot/cold
> **Il fait chaud en Inde. Il fait froid dans la cave.**
> *Ill fay shoh o-n A-nd. Ill fay frwa do-n lah cahv.*
> It's hot in India. It's cold in the cellar.

Forming Verb Tenses

To form the different verb tenses, we need to dive in a little deeper. To begin with, let's be clear on one crucial point: it is not necessary to know all the tenses. We are completely satisfied teaching you the basic necessities – those that you'll be using all the time: the present tense (which you'll use to form the future tense) and the **passé composé**, the most useful form of the past. These two tenses will enable you to get by quickly without having to study the other forms of the past or future tenses.

FAIRE LA GUEULE

Past Tense (passé composé)

Here's how the two tenses translate:

I speak	**je parle**	*jze parl*
I spoke	**j'ai parlé**	*jzay parlay*

Using the passé composé

Once you get the hang of how to form the **passé composé**, you'll feel liberated. Simply memorize the conjugation for the helping verbs, **être** (to be) and **avoir** (to have). Then add the main verb which you want to use with the easy ending **-é** or **-i**. And you've mastered the past tense in French.

être and avoir

je suis	(I am)	nous sommes	(we are)
j'ai	(I have)	nous avons	(we have)
tu es	(you are)	vous êtes	(you are)
tu as	(you have)	vous avez	(you have)
il, elle est	(he, she is)	ils, elles sont	(they are)
il, elle a	(he, she has)	ils, elles ont	(they have)

PLUS your choice of verb:

If you want to say that you ate (actually have eaten) a great **bouillabaisse** last night, simply plug in what we've just covered.

Hier soir j'ai mangé une bonne bouillabaisse.
Yair swar jzay mo-njzay oon bun booyuhbess.
Last night, I ate (have eaten) a great bouillabaisse.

Some verbs take the **être** (to be) helping verb but most take the **avoir** (to have) helping verb. When in doubt, use **avoir.** You'll catch on fast; don't panic. Note that verbs that imply movement or action almost always take **être.**

Forming the Past Participle
        -er verbs = é
        -ir verbs = i

You should note – but don't get overly concerned – that when **être** is used as the helping verb, the main verb changes according to person and gender. But not with **avoir.**

masculine: **Je suis arrivé à Paris.**
                    jze sweezareevay ah Paree.
                    I arrived in Paris.

feminine: **Je suis arrivée à Paris.**
                                           jze sweezareevay ah Paree.
                                           I arrived in Paris.

Forming the Future with the Present

We've already seen in detail the present tense used with the different verb groups. The simplest way to express a future action is to continue to use the present tense while adding phrases that imply the future.

- **dans une minute** (in a minute)	*do-nzoon meenoot*
- **dans une heure** (in an hour)	*do-nzoonuhr*
- **dans une semaine** (in a week)	*do-nzoon semen*
- **dans un mois** (in a month)	*do-nza-n mwa*
- **dans un an** (in a year)	*do-za-no-n*
- **tout à l'heure** (a little later)	*tootahluhr*
- **demain** (tomorrow)	*dema-n*
- **après-demain** (the day after tomorrow)	*ahpraydema-n*
- **dans trois jours** (in three days)	*do-ntrwah jzoor*
- **dans quinze jours** (in two weeks/15 days)	*do-n ka-nz jzoor*
- **demain soir** (tomorrow night)	*dema-n swar*
- **demain matin** (tomorrow morning)	*dema-n mahta-n*

Having clearly indicated when the action will take place, you use the verb conjugated in the present tense:

Ex: **Demain nous allons au cinéma.**
        Dema-n noosaloh-n oh cinayma.
        Tomorrow we go/are going to the cinema.

Ex: **Dans une semaine je suis en vacances.**
        Do-nzune semen jze sweezo-n vako-nce.
        In a week I am / I'll be on vacation.

This way of expressing a future action is commonly used in spoken French. The true future tense is somewhat more elegant, but to start with this shortcut is perfectly acceptable.

Negative Form

If you need to respond to a question in the negative, the easiest correct reply is simply "**non**" (no) or "**non, merci**" (no, thank you).

To create an entire sentence in the negative form you must use the structure "**ne**" + verb + "**pas**".

Tu es gentil.	**Tu n'es pas gentil.**
Too ay jzo-ntee.	*Too nay pah jzo-ntee.*
You are nice.	You are not nice.
Je parle français.	**Je ne parle pas français.**
Jze parl fro-nsay.	*Jze nuh parl pah fro-nsay.*
I speak French.	I do not speak French.
Elle a vingt ans.	**Elle n'a pas vingt ans.**
Elah va-nto-n.	*El nah pah va-nto-n.*
She is twenty years old.	She isn't twenty years old.

Note that **ne** becomes **n'** when it is followed by a word which begins with a vowel.

Other possible negative structures

ne... rien (nothing)	*nuh... reeye-n*
ne... jamais (never)	*nuh... jzamay*
ne... plus (no longer)	*nuh... ploo*
ne... personne (no one)	*nuh... pairsun*
ne... pas non plus (neither/not even)	*nuh... pah noh-n ploo*

Asking a Question

In French there are three ways to pose a question.

• The simplest is to repeat an affirmative statement while raising your voice at the end of the sentence.

Tu manges beaucoup.
Too mo-njz boh<u>koo</u>.
You eat a lot.

Tu manges beaucoup ?
Too mo-njz boh<u>koo</u> ?
Do you eat a lot?

• The second easiest – and most common – way is to start an affirmative statement with **est-ce que** (is it that...).

Est-ce que tu manges beaucoup ?
Eskuh too mo-njz boh<u>koo</u> ?
Do you eat a lot?

Il a raison.
Ill<u>ah</u> ray<u>zoh-n</u>.
He is right.

Est-ce qu'il a raison ?
Eskill<u>ah</u> ray<u>zoh-n</u> ?
Is he right?

Note again that **que** becomes **qu'** when the word that follows begins with a vowel.

• The third way to pose a question is the most literary and elegant. In general, chose this method when you want to be particularly polite. Take the affirmative and invert the verb and the personal pronoun. Note that this form of politeness goes with the **vous** form of **you**.

Tu parles français.
Too parl fro-nsay.
You speak French.

Parles-tu français ?
Parl too fro-n<u>say</u> ?
Do you speak French?

Vous connaissez un hôtel pas cher.
Voo connes<u>say</u> a-no<u>tel</u> pah <u>shair</u>.
You know a hotel not expensive.

Connaissez-vous un hôtel pas cher ?
Connessay <u>voo</u> a-notel pah shair ?
Do you know an inexpensive hotel?

CONNAISSEZ-VOUS UN HÔTEL PAS CHER ?

Key Words for Asking Questions

où ?	*oow*	where?
quoi ?	*kwa*	what?
quand ?	*ko-n*	when?
comment ?	*kom<u>mo-n</u>*	how?
combien ?	*koh-mbee<u>ye-n</u>*	how much?
qui ?	*kee*	who?
pourqoi ?	*poor<u>kwa</u>*	why?
combien de temps ?	*koh-mbee<u>ye-n</u> duh <u>to-n</u>*	how long?

Often all you need is the question word and **est-ce que** and the question asks itself.

Quand est-ce que le bus arrive ?
Ko-ntess kuh luh booss arreeve ?
When is the bus coming?

Pourquoi est-ce que tu ne dis rien ?
Poorkwa eskuh too nuh dee reeye-n ?
Why don't you say something?

Comment ça va ?
Kommo-n sah vah ?
How are you?

The Imperative

You won't need this tense very often, but it's a good idea to be familiar with it just in case. Here are a few examples.

Parle !	*Parl*	Speak!	**Parlez !**	*parlay*	Speak!
Viens !	*Veeye-n*	Come!	**Venez !**	*venay*	Come!
Vas-y !	*Vahzee*	Let's go!	**Allez-y !**	*ahlayzee*	Let's go!
Attends !	*Atto-n*	Wait!	**Attendez !**	*atto-nday*	Wait!

Prepositions

Prepositions, those seemingly easy "little" words, are often the most challenging to master. Try explaining to a French speaker the uses of to, from, at, on, in, etc. and you'll quickly see what we mean. Note that prepositions can't be translated directly.

The most important ones are **de** (of, from, about) and **à** (to, in, at). Don't confuse **à** the preposition and **a** the 3rd person singular conjugation of the verb **avoir**.

Je viens de Lyon.
Jze veeye-n duh Leeoh-n.
I come from Lyon.

Je vais à Nice.
Jze vay ah Neece.
I'm going to Nice

D'où viens-tu ?
Doo veeye-n too ?
Where do you come from?

Vous parlez de quoi ?
Voo parlay duh kwa ?
What are you talking about?

J'habite à Boston.
Jzabeet ah boston.
I live in Boston.

Other Prepositions

sur	*soor*	on	**sous**	*soo*	under
chez	*shay*	(house of)	**dans**	*do-n*	in
devant	*devo-n*	in front of	**derrière**	*darereeair*	behind
après	*ahpray*	after	**avant**	*ahvo-n*	before
avec	*ahvek*	with	**sans**	*so-n*	without
loin de	*lwa-n duh*	far from	**près de**	*pray duh*	nearby
au lieu de	*oh leeyuh duh*	instead of	**contre**	*coh-ntr*	against
			sauf	*sof*	except
depuis	*depwee*	since	**en**	*o-n*	in
entre	*o-ntre*	between	**jusqu'à**	*jzuskah*	until
malgré	*malgray*	despite	**par**	*par*	by
pendant	*po-nda-n*	during	**pour**	*poor*	for

Numbers and Measures

In French there are some differences in the way one counts. For example, 70, 80, and 90 are composed literally as *sixty-ten*, *four-twenty*, and *four-twenty-ten*, respectively. The number one **(un)** is masculine, but when it's used as the article before a noun it takes the gender of the noun, ex. **une voiture, un garçon**).

JE VIENS DE...

0	**zéro**	*zayroh*
1	**un, une**	*a-n, oon*
2	**deux**	*duh*
3	**trois**	*trwa*
4	**quatre**	*catr*
5	**cinq**	*sa-nk*
6	**six**	*siss*
7	**sept**	*set*
8	**huit**	*wheat*
9	**neuf**	*nuff*
10	**dix**	*diss*
11	**onze**	*oh-nz*
12	**douze**	*dooz*
13	**treize**	*trays*
14	**quatorze**	*catorz*
15	**quinze**	*ca-ns*
16	**seize**	*says*
17	**dix-sept**	*disset*

18	**dix-huit**	*deez<u>wheat</u>*
19	**dix-neuf**	*deez<u>nuff</u>*
20	**vingt**	*va-n*
21	**vingt et un**	*va-ntey<u>a-n</u>*
22	**vingt-deux**	*va-nt<u>duh</u>*
23	**vingt-trois**	*va-nt<u>trwa</u>*
30	**trente**	*tro-nt*
40	**quarante**	*car<u>o-nt</u>*
50	**cinquante**	*sa-n<u>ko-nt</u>*
60	**soixante**	*swa<u>sso-nt</u>*
70	**soixante-dix**	*swasso-nt <u>diss</u>*
71	**soixante et onze**	*swasso-ntay<u>oh-nz</u>*
72	**soixante-douze**	*swasso-nt<u>dooz</u>*
80	**quatre-vingt**	*catre<u>va-n</u>*
81	**quatre-vingt-un**	*catreva-n <u>a-n</u>*
90	**quatre-vingt-dix**	*catreva-n <u>diss</u>*
97	**quatre-vingt-dix-sept**	*catreva-n dis<u>set</u>*
100	**cent**	*so-n*
101	**cent un**	*so-n a-n*
111	**cent onze**	*so-n oh-nz*
180	**cent quatre-vingt**	*so-n catre<u>va-n</u>*
200	**deux cent**	*duh so-n*
300	**trois cent**	*trwa so-n*
1000	**mille**	*mill*
1100	**mille cent**	*mill <u>so-n</u>*
1200	**mille deux cent**	*mill duh <u>so-n</u>*
10.000	**dix mille**	*deemill*
100.000	**cent mille**	*so-n mill*
1.000.000	**un million**	*a-n mil<u>yoh-n</u>*

Note that with numbers the French system uses commas where the Anglo-Saxon uses decimal points, and vice versa.

Ex.   1.000.000,50 (French)
             1,000,000.50 (English)

Ordinal Numbers

premier	1er	*premiyeah*	first
première	1re	*premiyair*	first
deuxième	2e	*duhzeeyem*	second
troisième	3e	*trwazeeyem*	third
quatrième	4e	*catreeyem*	fourth
centième	100e	*so-ntyem*	hundredth
une fois		*oon fwa*	once
deux fois		*duh fwa*	twice
trois fois		*trwa fwa*	three times
quelquefois		*kelkuhfwa*	sometimes

Measures

Note that the French, like most people in the world, use the metric system. If you come from the United States, this will take some getting used to. Quickly, there are four liters to a gallon, 500 grams make a pound, 2.2 pounds equal a kilo, 39 centimeters make up a yard, and a kilometer is 0.6 miles.

un litre	*a-n leetr*	liter
une livre	*a-n leevr*	pound(500 grams)
cent grammes	*so-n gram*	100 grams
un demi-litre	*a-n demi leetr*	1/2 liter
un kilo	*a-n keelo*	kilo
une paire	*oon pair*	a pair
quelques	*kelkuh*	a few
une douzaine	*oon douzayn*	a dozen
la moitié	*la mwatiyeh*	half
un quart	*a-n cahr*	a quarter
un tiers	*a-n tiyair*	a third
le double	*luh doobl*	double
un morceau	*a-n morsoh*	a piece

Indicators of Time

A Sampling

le jour	*luh jzoor*	the day
la semaine	*lah semen*	the week
le mois	*luh mwa*	the month
l'an	*lo-n*	the year
neuf mois	*nuff mwa*	nine months
trois mois	*trwa mwa*	three months
la date	*lah daht*	the date
hier	*yair*	yesterday
demain	*dema-n*	tomorrow
après-demain	*ahpray dema-n*	the day after tomorrow
aujourd'hui	*ohjzoor 'dwee*	today
le week-end	*le weekend*	the weekend
il y a deux jours	*illeeyah duh jzoor*	two days ago
la semaine prochaine	*lah semmen proshen*	next week
quinze jours	*ca-nz jzoor*	two weeks

Parts of the Day

le matin	*luh mata-n*	morning
le midi	*luh middee*	noon
à midi	*ah middee*	at noon
l'après-midi	*lahpreymiddee*	afternoon
le soir	*luh swar*	evening
la nuit	*lah nwee*	night, at night
minuit	*minwee*	midnight
à minuit	*ah minwee*	at midnight

42

Days of the Week

dimanche	*deemo-nsh*	Sunday
lundi	*la-ndee*	Monday
mardi	*mardee*	Tuesday
mercredi	*maircredee*	Wednesday
jeudi	*jzuhdee*	Thursday
vendredi	*vo-ndredee*	Friday
samedi	*sammdee*	Saturday

Months of the Year

janvier	*jzo-nveeay*	January
février	*fevreeay*	February
mars	*mahrss*	March
avril	*ahvrill*	April
mai	*may*	May
juin	*jzewa-n*	June
juillet	*jzuyeah*	July
août	*oowt*	August
septembre	*septo-mbr*	September
octobre	*octobr*	October
novembre	*novo-mbr*	November
décembre	*daysso-mbr*	December

The Seasons

le printemps / au printemps	*luh pra-nto-n* / *oh pra-nto-n*	spring / in springtime
l'été / en été	*lettay* / *o-nettay*	summer / in summertime
l'automne / en...	*lohton* / *o-nohton*	autumn / in the fall
l'hiver / en...	*leevair* / *o-neevair*	winter / in wintertime
la saison	*lah sayzoh-n*	the season

43

Dates

In French, dates are always given with the day of the month first, the month second, and the year last. The article **le** always precedes the date.

le 15 avril 1968   **le 5 octobre 2000**

On est le combien aujourd'hui ?
O-nay luh koh-mbee<u>ye-n</u> ohjzoor<u>dwee</u> ?
What's today's date?

Nous sommes le cinq mars.
Noo <u>sum</u> luh sa-nk <u>mahrss</u>.
It's March 5th.

Quelle est votre date de naissance ?
Kellay vohtr <u>dat</u> duh nay<u>sso-n</u>ss ?
What's your date of birth?

Je suis né le onze mai mille neuf cent cinquante.
Jze swee <u>nay</u> luh <u>oh-nz</u> <u>mill</u> meal nuff so-n sa-n<u>ko-nt</u>.
I was born on May 11th 1950.

Quel âge as-tu ?   **J'ai vingt ans.**
Kel<u>jajz</u> ah <u>too</u> ?   *Jzay va-n<u>to-n</u>.*
How old are you?   I'm twenty.

Time

In French **l'heure** is the word used for both hour and o'clock. The French use the 24-hour clock.

l'heure	*luhr*	hour, o'clock
la minute	*lah mi<u>noot</u>*	minute
la seconde	*la se<u>goh-nd</u>*	second

demi	*demi*	half
une demi-heure	*oon demi-<u>uhr</u>*	a half hour
quart	*cahr*	quarter
un quart d'heure	*a-n cahr <u>duhr</u>*	a quarter of an hour
moins	*mwa-n*	to (the hour)

Quelle heure est-il ?
Kelluhr ay<u>teel</u> ?
What time is it?

Il est tard / tôt.
Illay <u>tahr</u> / <u>toh</u>.
It's late / early.

À quelle heure ?
Ah kel<u>luhr</u> ?
At what time?

Il est neuf heures dix.
Illay nuhvuhr <u>diss</u>.
It's nine o'clock.

Je viens demain soir.
Jze vee<u>ye-n</u> dema-n <u>swar</u>.
I am coming tomorrow night.

À huit heures.
Ah wheat-<u>uhr</u>.
At 8 o'clock.

QUELLE HEURE EST-IL ?

À tout à l'heure.
Ah tootah<u>luhr</u>.
See you later.

Je reviens tout de suite.
Jze reveeye-n <u>tood</u> <u>sweet</u>.
I'll be right back..

Quand venez-vous ?
Ko-n venay <u>voo</u> ?
When are you coming?

Dans une heure ?
Do-nzoon<u>uhr</u> ?
In an hour?

10.00 o'clock	**dix heures (du matin)**	*deezuhr (doo mata-n)*
11.05	**onze heures cinq**	*oh-nzuhr sa-nk*
12.15	**midi et quart**	*mid<u>dee</u> ay cahr*
1.25	**une heure vingt-cinq**	*oon uhr va-n sa-nk*
2.30	**deux heures et demie**	*duh zuhr ay de<u>mee</u>*
3.35	**quatre heures moins vingt-cinq**	*cattr uhr mwa-n va-ntsa-nk*
6.45	**sept heures moins le quart**	*setuhr mwa-n luh <u>cahr</u>*
7.50	**huit heures moins dix**	*wheat<u>uhr</u> mwa-n diss*
8.55	**neuf heures moins cinq**	*nuh<u>yuhr</u> mwa-n sank*
00.10	**minuit dix**	*min<u>wee</u> diss*

The Weather

Il fait beau.
Ill fay <u>boh</u>.
It's nice out.

Il fait froid.
Ill fay <u>frwa</u>.
It's cold out.

Il fait ...	*ill fay*	It's ...
... frais	*fray*	... cool
... humide	*oo<u>meed</u>*	... wet/damp
... doux	*doo*	... mild
... beau / mauvais	*boh / moh<u>vay</u>*	... nice/nasty
... bon	*boh-n*	... fine
Il y a ...	*Illeeyah*	It's...
... du vent	*doo <u>vo-n</u>*	... windy
... du brouillard	*doo bruee<u>are</u>*	... foggy

46

Quelle chaleur !		**Il pleut / il neige.**
Kel shalluhr !		*Ill pluh / ill naijz.*
What heat!		It's raining / it's snowing.

l'orage	*lorrahjz*	storm
le verglas	*luh vairglah*	frost
le ciel	*luh seeyel*	sky
la lune	*lah loon*	moon
le brouillard	*luh brueeare*	fog
le nord	*luh nor*	North
l'est	*lest*	East
l'ouest	*lwest*	West
le sud	*luh sood*	South
la pluie	*lah plwee*	rain
la neige	*lah naijz*	snow
le soleil	*luh solay*	sun
les étoiles	*laysetwal*	stars
le vent	*luh vo-n*	wind
la météo	*lah mehteyoh*	weather forecast
le temps	*luh to-n*	weather
le nuage	*luh nuajz*	cloud

Directions / Places

Here is a useful list of words you'll need when asking and receiving directions.

à droite	*ah drwat*	right
à gauche	*ah gosh*	left
tout droit	*tu drwa*	straight ahead
en haut	*o-n oh*	up, above
en bas	*o-n bah*	down, below
ici	*eecee*	here
là	*lah*	here, there
là-bas	*lahbah*	over there
au coin	*oh kwa-n*	at the corner

Geography

Départements and Regions in France

France's political geography is divided into 95 **départements** and twenty **regions**. Each region consists of a cluster of **départements**. The **départements** are numbered, and these numbers are used as the first two digits of each town's postal code and as the last two digits of French license plates. Paris, its own **département**, takes the number 75. Here is the list of geographic regions.

l'Alsace-Lorraine	*lalsas-lorrain*
l'Anjou	*lo-njzoo*
l'Aquitaine	*lackeetayn*
l'Auvergne	*lovairnye*
le Berry	*luh berree*
la Bourgogne	*lah boorgunye*
la Bretagne	*lah bretanye*
la Champagne	*lah sho-mpahnye*
la Gascogne	*lah gascohnye*
l'Ile de France	*leel duh fro-ns*
le Languedoc	*luh lo-nguedoc*
le Limousin	*luh limooza-n*
le Midi	*luh middee*
la Normandie	*lah normo-ndee*
le Périgord	*luh pereegor*
la Picardie	*lah picardee*
le Poitou	*luh pwatoo*
la Provence	*lah provo-ns*
le Roussillon	*luh roosseeyoh-n*
la Touraine	*lah toorren*

Où vas-tu cet été ?
Oow vah too set etay ?
Where are you going this summer?

Je vais dans le Midi.
Jze vay do-n luh middee.
I'm going to the south of France.

Countries and Nationalities

The names of countries are usually feminine in French and thus are preceded by the article **la**, like **la France**. Here's a list of countries in French with the word form used to describe their citizens and the corresponding adjective.

les États-Unis	*layzaytahzoonee*	United States
les Étasuniens	*layzaytahzoonye-n*	} Americans
les Américains	*layzamayreeka-n*	
étasunien / étasunienne	*aytahzoonye-n / aytahzoonyenn*	} American
américain / américaine	*amayreeka-n / amayreekenn*	
la Grande Bretagne	*lah gro-nd bretanye*	Great Britain
les Britanniques	*lay breetan<u>neek</u>*	British
anglais / anglaise	*o-n<u>glay</u> / o-n<u>glayz</u>*	English
le Canada	*luh cahnah<u>dah</u>*	Canada
les Canadiens	*lay cahnah<u>dye-n</u>*	Canadians
canadien / canadienne	*cahnah<u>dye-n</u> / cahnah<u>dyenn</u>*	Canadian
l'Australie	*lostrah<u>lee</u>*	Australia
les Australiens	*layzostrah<u>lye-n</u>*	Australians
australien / australienne	*ostrah<u>lye-n</u> / ostrah<u>lyenn</u>*	Australian
la Suisse	*lah swiss*	Switzerland
les Suisses	*lay swiss*	Swiss
suisse / suisse	*swiss / swiss*	Swiss
la France	*lah fro-ns*	France
les Français	*lay fro-n<u>say</u>*	French
français / française	*fro-n<u>say</u> / fro-n<u>sez</u>*	French
la Belgique	*lah belljzeek*	Belgium
les Belges	*lay belljz*	Belgians
belge / belge	*belljz / belljz*	Belgian

D'où viens-tu ?	**Je viens de Suisse / d'Algérie.**
Doo veeye-n too ?	*Jze veeye-n duh swiss / daljze<u>ree</u>.*
Where do you come from?	I come from Spain/Algeria.

Congratulations! You've reached the end of the grammatical portion of this book. Let's talk.

CONVERSATION

A Mini-Guide to the French and Their Habits

It is always dangerous trying to characterize or stereotype any one group of people. However, there are always a few general characteristics that tend to be true, which can be useful in understanding local attitudes and behaviour. Whereas it is said that North Americans tend to be open and friendly, it can be said that the French tend to be more formal and reserved. If you say **bonjour** to a stranger on the streets of Paris, don't be surprised if you don't get a response. This is not an act of rudeness; if anything, you may be perceived as being impolite or weird in that in general you don't address people you don't know.

In France, form is everything – from the structure of a meal to the way you ask for directions. So keep a keen eye out for not only what people do and say, but how they do it and how they say it. Regarding language, use the formal **vous** as a rule. When addressing someone, always begin with a slow and polite **Bonjour, Monsieur** or **Bonjour, Madame** and wait till you've been acknowledged before asking your question.

Note that the French always greet people they know and/or work with by shaking hands or giving a succession of two, three, or four little kisses on alternating cheeks, an act called **faire la bise**. Observe and replicate.

You'll probably hear in the streets certain words that you can't find in the dictionary. These are colloquial expressions or specialized slang words called **l'argot.** Start your own list of these words as you hear them in that they are your passport to daily street life, but caution is advised. Don't use **argot** before you are sure of the meaning and the context.

Here are two simple structures that you'll use endlessly when initiating conversation.

Pourriez-vous..., s'il vous plaît. **Je voudrais...**
Poorryeh<u>voo</u> seelvoo<u>play</u> *Jze voodray...*
Could you please... I would like...

The Language of Gestures

You've already been introduced to **la bise**. French people are often very expressive and use all sorts of body language and facial gestures to communicate. Some say that when asked a question the French alway begin their reply by pursing their lips. In fact the French mouth does a lot more than speak, and as you observe closely you'll begin to master the movements, sounds, and meanings. For example, a spritzing sound is the French equivalent of the Anglo-Saxon shrug of the shoulders. Often accompanied or followed by the very French expression **tant pis**, uttered when there is nothing to do about a situation and a philosophic burst of resignation is called for, another way of saying **C'est comme ça**, it's just like that; don't fight it. Compliance may be less principled but it's also less painful.

Slightly pulling down the skin below the right eye with the right pointer finger is the gestural translation of **mon œil**, my eye, a bit of common sarcasm meaning "sure, right, I don't believe you for a second."

The common gesture of disbelief or amazement is the rapid shaking of the hand bent at the wrist, accompanied with the universal **oh la la**!

Superlative adjectives these days include: **super** and **hyper**. An old standby is **chouette,** the French version of cool, neat.

Other Onomatopeias in French

aïe !	_a-ii_	ouch!
berk !	_bairk_	yuck!
bof !	_bof_	nah!
oh la la !	_oh lah lah_	wow, yippie!
zut !	_zoot_	damn it!

First Contact

In France, first impressions are vital and they set the tone for the relationships that you will have. Be prepared to be judged by the way you dress, the way you speak, the way you act. So, it's always better to get it right from the start and not make too many **faux pas**. As a rule, don't overlook the details, form, and aesthetics. Use the **vous** form and don't switch into the **tu**, although the French generally understand that this is tough for English speakers. And even though they won't admit it, they sometimes give the impression that they're envious of your ease at familiarity. Here are some conversational tips that will help you make that first contact and assist you in replying to questions that you'll most likely be asked.

Bonjour.
boh-njzoor
Hello.

Enchanté(e)
o-nsho-ntay
Nice to meet you.

Bonjour, comment ça va ?
boh-njzoor, kommo-n sah vah ?
Hello, how are you?.

Ça va bien, merci. Et vous ?
Sah vah beeye-n, mairsee, ay voo?
Fine thank you. And you?

Comment vous appelez-vous ?
Kommo-n voozahpelay voo ?
What's your name?

Je m'appelle Karen.
Jze mahpell Karen.
My name is Karen.

D'où viens-tu ?
Doo veeye-n too ?
Where do you come from?

Je viens du Canada.
Jze veeye-n doo Cahnahdah.
I come from Canada.

De quelle ville ?
Duh kell veel ?
From which city?

De Vancouver.
Duh Vancoovair.
From Vancouver.

Je ne connais pas.
Jze nuh cunnay pah.
I've never been there.

Où est-ce ?
Oow ehs ?
Where is it?

After this first conversation, you might wish to get to know the person better. Here's how to set up a rendez-vous or at least suggest that you expect to see the person again.

À tout à l'heure.
Ah tootaluhr.
See you later.

À demain.
Ah dema-n.
Till tomorrow.

Je vais repasser.
Jze vay repassay.
I'll stop by again.

Je vous téléphone.
Jze voo telayphone.
I'll call you.

Je propose...
Jze propose...
I propose...

Je voudrais...
Jze voodray...
I would like...

J'espère vous revoir.
Jzespair voo revwar.
I hope to see you again.

Vous avez des projets pour demain ?
Voozavay day projzay poor dema-n ?
Do you have plans for tomorrow?

Quand est-ce que vous êtes à la maison ?
Ko-ntess kuh voozet ah lah maysoh-n.
When will you be home?

On va au cinéma / boire un pot ?
Oh-n vah oh cinayma / bwar a-n poh ?
How about going to the cinema / How about going for a drink?

Avec plaisir.
Ahvec playzeer.
With pleasure.

D'accord.
Dakcor.
Okay./In accord.

Je n'ai pas envie.
Jze nay pahzo-nvee.
I don't feel like it.

Pas question !
Pah kesteeho-n.
No way!

At Home / With the Family

la famille	*lah fahmee*	family
la femme	*lah fahm*	wife
le mari	*luh marree*	husband
le fils	*luh feece*	son
la fille	*lah fee*	daughter
la tante	*lah to-nt*	aunt
l'oncle	*loh-nkl*	uncle
le grand-père	*luh gro-npare*	grandfather
la grand-mère	*lah gro-nmare*	grandmother
un ami	*a-nahmee*	friend (male)
une amie	*oonahmee*	friend (female)
le père	*luh pare*	father
la mère	*lah mare*	mother
les parents	*lay pahro-n*	parents
les grands-parents	*lay gro-npahro-n*	grandparents
les petits-enfants	*lay peteezo-nfo-n*	grandchildren

54

marié(e)	*mareeyeh*	married
fiancé(e)	*feeno-nseh*	engaged
célibataire	*seleebahtare*	single
divorcé(e)	*deevorseh*	divorced
veuf / veuve	*vuhf / vuv*	widower/widow

A Note on Marital Status

In France it is not uncommon for couples to live together for a long time or forever without getting married, even after having children. There is absolutely no moral or societal stigma to this, and in fact the practice is openly called **concubinage** or more recently **vie maritale** (married life).

Soyez la bienvenue !
Swayeh la beeye-nvenoo !
Welcome!

Soyez le bienvenu !
Swayeh luh beeye-nvenoo !
Welcome!

Entrez !
O-ntray
Come in!

Asseyez-vous !
Ahssayeh-voo !
Sit down (Have a seat!)

Vous êtes l'ami(e) de Jean ?
Voozet lahmee duh Jzo-n ?
You are Jean's friend?

Oui, c'est moi.
Wee say mwah.
Yes, that's me.

Quelle est votre profession ?
Kellay vohtr professeeyoh-n ?
What kind of work do you do?

Je suis avocat(e) / employé(e).
Jze swee ahvocah(t) / o-nplwayeh.
I am a lawyer / employee.

Je suis étudiant(e).
Jze sweez ehtoodio-n(t).
I am a student.

Qu'est-ce que vous faites comme études ?
keskuh voo fet cum etood ?
What are you studying?

Je fais des études d'histoire / d'anglais.
Jze fay dayzetood distwar / do-nglay.
I am studying history / English.

Vous désirez boire quelque chose ?
Voo dayziray bwar kelkuh shows ?
Would you like something to drink?

Ça vous plaît la France ?
Sah voo play, la fro-ns ?
Do you like France?

Oui, beaucoup.
weei bohkoo.
Yes, a lot.

le nom	*luh noh-m*	last name
le prénom	*luh praynho-m*	first name
la famille	*lah fahmee*	family
la maison	*lah mayzoh-n*	house
le jardin	*luh jzarda-n*	garden
l'appartement	*lappartemo-n*	apartment
la chambre	*lah sho-mbr*	bedroom
la cuisine	*lah queezeene*	kitchen
la salle de bains	*lah sall duh ba-n*	bathroom
les toilettes	*lay twalet*	toilet

A Note on Bathrooms

In French houses and apartments, the toilet is usually in a separate, small room, nearby but detached from the room in which the bath and sink are located. The toilet is commonly called the WC (*ley vey say*). Utilities and appliances tend to be considerably smaller than their North American counterparts.

If you are accustomed to American-style showers, be prepared for hilarious moments of acrobatic hygiene as French showers often consist of a hand-held nozzle, which means you never have more than one hand free.

Working in France

There is much to be said about the work culture in France, but in that you are probably in France for fun and pleasure, only a brief glance at the key vocabulary should be necessary.

le travail	*luh travaii*	work
la profession	*lah professeeyoh-n*	profession
Je suis ...	*jze swee*	I am a...
étudiant(e)	*ehtoodio-n(t)*	university student
lycéen(ne)	*leesaya-n (leesayen)*	high school student
élève	*ellev*	pupil, grade school student
chômeur (chômeuse)	*showmuhr (showmuhz)*	unemployed person
ouvrier (ouvrière)	*oovreeyeh (oovreeyair)*	worker
employé(e)	*o-nplwayeh*	employee
technicien(ne)	*techniseeye-n (technisseeyen)*	technician
apprenti(e)	*appro-ntee*	trainee

artiste	*arteest*	artist
commerçant(e)	*comairso-n(t)*	merchant
retraité(e)	*reytretay*	retiree
fonctionnaire	*funcseeyonair*	state employee
cadre	*cadr*	middle manager / junior executive
cadre superieur	*cadr supaireeyuhr*	upper manager

Eating in France

Almost everything in France revolves around the table – conversation, work, leisure, social life... Get used to long meals. And even after you have coasted through the **apéritif,** the entrée, the plat principal, salad, a cheese course, plenty of very decent wine, and two desserts don't get ready to get up. There will be fruit and then coffee, perhaps some chocolates and certainly a **digestif** like cognac or Calvados. And cigarettes and cigars and another coffee... and plenty of talk. What is enchanting about this ritual is the degree of dialog you'll be exposed to.

The rhythm and form of the dinner meal must be learned and mastered. To have a successful stay in France don't be too insistent on old habits when it comes to eating. In restaurants, if you split an appetizer or skip dessert don't be alarmed if the waiter seems intolerant. **C'est comme ça !** You're violating the code.

Briefly, **le petit déjeuner**, breakfast, consists of **café au lait** or tea, bread **(baguette),** butter, jam. **Croissants** or **pains au chocolat** are served in hotels and cafés.

Lunch can range from a ham sandwich to a full, three-course spread. If you plan on eating a real meal at lunch time, make sure you get yourself seated before 2 p.m. (14h), in that no one serves later than that. You can always grab a snack or **croque-monsieur** in a *café* but the French don't consider that really eating.

L'ARTISTE

Dinner is usually not served before 8 p.m. Cocktails *(apéritifs)* are always offered. If you are lost for what to order, ask for a **kir**, white wine and a dash of ***crème de cassis*** (black currant liquor). Popular and tasty.

If you are invited to someone's home in France it will almost always be for a meal. Dress slightly more formal than you'd think of doing back home. And never show up empty-handed. Flowers are always appreciated but tell the florist that they're a gift. He or she will wrap them to give, as opposed to the plainer paper you get when you're just taking the flowers home. A bottle of champagne is always appreciated. If you bring a bottle of wine make sure it's a good one. Table wine, inexpensive wines, and the ones with the blue metal wrapper over the cork will not win you any points with your hosts.

Even in the heat of summer the French generally would not show up at someone else's lawn party in shorts and a pitcher of lemonade. Take that as a cue.

Don't get worried if the **apéritif** hour takes two. This is normal. When your hosts are ready they'll invite everyone "**à table**". Don't forget that the **entrée** in France is the starter dish, not the main dish as the Americans call it. If you need a few compliments for the chef:

C'est très bon !	*say tray boh-n*	It's very good.
C'est délicieux !	*say delissee-uh*	It's delicious.
C'est magnifique !	*say mahnyeefik*	It's magnificent.

J'aime bien la soupe.
Jzem bee<u>ye</u>-n lah <u>soop</u>.
I like the soup a lot.

Comment c'est fait ?
Kom<u>mo-n</u> say <u>fay</u> ?
How do you make it?

Getting Around in France

Here are a few questions that will be useful when you need to get somewhere.

Pour aller à..., s'il vous plaît ?
Poor al<u>lay</u> ah... seel voo <u>play</u> ?
How does one get to..., please?

C'est à combien de kilomètres ?
Settah co-mbee<u>ye</u>-n duh keelo<u>maitr</u> ?
How many kilometers is it?

Je cherche..., s'il vous plaît.
Jze shairsh..., seel voo <u>play</u>.
I am looking for ..., please.

Où se trouve... ?
Oow suh troov...
Where can I find...?

... by Public Transportation

Un aller deuxième classe pour La Rochelle, s'il vous plaît.
A-nallay doozeeyem class poor Larowshell, seel voo play.
A one-way ticket, second class, for La Rochelle, please.

Il y a un tarif réduit pour étudiants ?
Illeeyah a-n tahreef raydwee poor ehtoodeeo-n ?
Is there a reduced rate for students?

Où est-ce que je dois changer ?
Oow eskuh jze dwa sho-njay ?
Where must I change?

Quand est-ce que le train arrive à Toulouse ?
Ko-nteskuh luh tra-n arreev ah Toolooz ?
When does the train get to Toulouse?

Est-ce qu'il y a une correspondance pour Nîmes ?
Eskeelleeyah oon correspoh-ndo-ns poor Neem ?
Is there a connecting train for Nîmes?

The French national train network is called the SNCF. You can go to practically any town in the entire country by train, and the major cities are served by the famous, high-speed wonder, the TGV (**train à grande vitesse**).

EST-CE QU'IL Y A UNE CORRESPONDANCE POUR...

In Paris, the mass transit system is called the RATP, which includes the **Métro** (subway), the commuter rail system called the RER, and the bus lines. Public transport is excellent, relatively safe and inexpensive. For short stays, your best bet is buying a **carnet** of ten tickets good for all **Métro** and bus travel. The monthly pass, **Carte Orange**, is highly economical for stays of a month or more.

A Few Key Questions

Où est la Gare de Lyon, s'il vous plaît ?
Oow <u>ay</u> lah gahr duh Lee<u>oh-n</u>, seeh voo <u>play</u> ?
Where is the Gare de Lyon train station, please?

Où est l'arrêt du bus numéro 24 ?
Oow <u>ay</u> lar<u>ray</u> doo <u>boos</u> noomairoh va-nt<u>catr</u> ?
Where is the stop for the Number 24 bus?

Quel bus va aux Champs-Élysées ?
Kel boos vah oh Cho-nzeleesay ?
Which bus goes to the Champs-Elysées?

Où est-ce que je dois descendre ?
Oow eskuh jze dwa desso-ndr ?
Where should I get off?

Où pourrais-je trouver un taxi ?
Oow poorrayjze troovay a-n taxi ?
Where can I find a taxi?

descendre	*desso-ndr*	to descend, get off
monter	*moh-ntay*	to mount, get on
changer	*sho-njzay*	to change
l'horaire	*lorair*	schedule
la réservation	*lah reyservahseeyoh-n*	reservations
le billet	*luh beeyeah*	ticket
le supplément	*luh sooplehmo-n*	supplement
l'aller	*lallay*	one-way
le retour	*luh retoor*	return
aller-retour	*allay-retoor*	round-trip
le départ	*luh daypar*	departure
l'arrivée	*lareevay*	arrival
l'arrêt	*larray*	stop
la correspondance	*lah correspoh-ndo-ns*	connection
la destination	*lah desteenahseeyoh-n*	destination
la sortie de secours	*lah sortee duh sekoor*	emergency exit
les bagages	*lay bahgahjz*	baggage
le séjour	*luh sayjzoor*	stay
la gare	*lah gahr*	station
le train	*luh tra-n*	train
la station	*lah stahseeyoh-n*	station
le guichet	*luh geeshay*	ticket window

la salle d'attente	*lah sahl dahto-nt*	waiting room
la voie	*lah vwah*	track
le compartiment	*luh coh-mparteemo-n*	compartment
le contrôleur	*luh coh-ntroluhr*	ticket-taker
les couchettes	*lay cooshet*	sleeping car
le quai	*luh kay*	platform
l'aéroport	*lah-ayropohr*	airport
l'avion	*lahveeoh-n*	airplane
le vol	*luh voll*	flight
le bateau	*luh bahto*	boat
le bus, le car	*luh boos, luh cahr*	bus, coach
le camion	*luh cameeoh-n*	truck
la mobylette	*lah mobeelet*	motorbike
la moto	*lah motoh*	motorcycle
le véhicule	*luh vayheecool*	vehicle
le vélo	*luh vayloh*	bike
faire de l'auto-stop	*fair duh lohto stup*	to hitchhike

... by car

la voiture	*la vwatur*	car
conduire	*coh-ndweer*	to drive
l'autoroute	*lotoroot*	highway
le péage	*luh payahjz*	toll booth
l'embouteillage	*lo-mbootayahjz*	traffic jam
l'essence	*lesso-ns*	gasoline
sans plomb	*so-n plho-n*	lead-free
la station-service	*lah stahseeyoh-n sairveece*	service station
la vitesse	*lah veetess*	speed
la limite de vitesse	*lah limeet de veetess*	speed limit
le permis de conduire	*luh pairmee duh coh-ndweer*	driver's license

le PV,	*luh payvay*	ticket
la contravention	*lah coh-ntrahvo-nseeyoh-n*	
le stationnement	*luh stahceeonnmo-n*	parking
le parking	*luh parking*	parking lot
la plaque	*lah plak*	license plate
d'immatriculation	*dimatricoolahseeyoh-n*	

Street Signs

ARRÊT INTERDIT	No Stopping
ATTENTION	Watch Out!
CHAUSSÉE DÉFORMÉE	Soft Shoulder
DANGER	Danger
DÉVIATION	Detour
RALENTIR	Slow
SENS INTERDIT	One Way
STATIONNEMENT INTERDIT	No Parking
VIRAGES	Bend

Driving in France can be a true adventure. First of all, the rule of the road is **la priorité à droite**, which means that the car to your right always has priority and unless otherwise indicated, you must yield. Drivers tend to be fast and aggressive, but surprisingly not as angry or nasty as their North American counterparts. Parking can be extremely difficult in Paris and the fleet of meter maids is never far off. Parking tickets begin at 75 F!

Avoid the French roads on the major holidays and the beginning and ending of the summer vacation periods in that all the major arteries are seriously clogged. Note that the French tend to all go to the same places at the same time, especially the mountains and the seashore in the month of August. The super highways, **autoroutes,** are toll roads, but the national highways, marked by the letter N, are free and more scenic, although slower.

Here are a few tips for communicating on the road:

Le plein, s'il vous plaît !
Luh pla-n, seel voo play !
Fill 'er up, please!

Pourriez-vous vérifier l'huile ?
Poorreeay voo vairifeeyeh lwheel ?
Could you check the oil?

Où est-ce qu'il y a une station-service, s'il vous plaît ?
Oow eskilleeyah oon stahseeyoh-n sairvees, seel vous play ?
Where's a service station, please?

Où est-ce que je peux garer ma voiture ?
Oow eskuh jze puh garray mah vwatur ?
Where can I park my car?

C'est bien la route de Marseille ?
Say beeye-n lah root duh Marsaii ?
Is this the right road to Marseille?

Je voudrais louer une voiture.
Jze voodray looway oon vwatur.
I'd like to rent a car.

Out of Order / Breaking Down

It's never fun having car problems or running out of gas, so you should be at least equipped with some vocabulary if this should happen to you in the French-speaking world.

le service de dépannage	*luh sairvees duh daypahnnajz*	roadside service
l'axe	*lax*	axis
le démarreur	*luh dehmarruhr*	starter

le tuyau d'échappement	*luh tweeyoh dehshapmo-n*	tailpipe
la batterie	*lah battree*	battery
les freins	*lay fra-n*	brakes
la pression	*lah presseeyoh-n*	tire pressure
les pièces de rechange	*lay peeyess duh resho-nzj*	spare parts
le défaut	*luh dehfoh*	faulty
la vitesse	*lah veetess*	gear
la carrosserie	*lah cahrosseree*	chassis
la courroie	*lah coorwa*	fan belt
le piston	*luh peestoh-n*	piston
le radiateur	*luh rahdeeahtuhr*	radiator
l'embrayage	*lo-mbrayajz*	clutch
le volant	*luh volo-n*	steering wheel
la dynamo	*lah deenamoh*	dynamo
le moteur	*luh mohtuhr*	motor
l'huile	*lweel*	oil
la vidange	*lah veedo-njz*	oil change
la roue	*lah rooh*	wheel
le pneu	*luh pnuh*	tire
réparer	*rayparray*	to repair
le phare	*luh fahr*	headlight
l'amortisseur	*lamorteessuhr*	shock absorber
le pare-chocs	*luh parshuk*	bumper
l'accident	*laxeedo-n*	accident
le carburateur	*luh carboohrahtuhr*	carburator
le cric	*luh creek*	jack
les outils	*layzootee*	tools
le pare-brise	*luh par breez*	windshield/windscreen
la bougie	*lah boojzee*	spark plug
le cylindre	*luh seela-ndr*	cylinder

Ma voiture est en panne.
Mah vwatur ehto-n pahn.
My car isn't working.

MA VOITURE EST EN PANNE.

Ma voiture ne démarre pas.
Mah vwa<u>tur</u> nuh day<u>mar</u> <u>pah</u>.
My car won't start.

Pourriez-vous réparer ma voiture ?
Pooreeay <u>voo</u> raypar<u>ray</u> mah vwa<u>tur</u> ?
Can you repair my car?

Ça dure combien de temps ?
Sah door co-mbee<u>ye-n</u> duh <u>to-n</u> ?
How long will it take?

Avez-vous des pièces de rechange ?
Ahvay voo day peeyess duh resha-njz ?
Do you have spare parts?

Il y a eu un accident.
Illeeyah ew a-nnaxeedo-n.
There has been an accident.

Pourriez-vous me remorquer ?
Pooreeay voo muh remorkay ?
Can you tow me?

Lodging

As you already know, almost everyone in France goes on vacation in either July or August. If you are planning to travel during these months, it is strongly advised that you reserve ahead. Otherwise, you are likely to be met everywhere with the word **complet** (*co-mplay*), full, no vacancy.

At the Hotel

l'hôtel	*lohtel*	hotel
complet	*coh-mplay*	full
la réception	*lah raycepseeyoh-n*	reception
la clé	*lah clay*	key
l'ascenseur	*lassensuhr*	elevator
l'étage	*lettajz*	floor
la chambre	*lah sho-mbr*	room
le chauffage	*luh shohfahjz*	heat
la climatisation	*lah cleemateezasseeyoh-n*	air conditioning
la fenêtre	*lah fennetr*	window
la lampe	*lah lo-mp*	lamp
la prise	*lah preez*	outlet, plug
le courant	*luh cooro-n*	current

69

la salle de bains	*lah sahl duh <u>ba-n</u>*	bathroom
la douche	*lah doosh*	shower
le lavabo	*luh lahvah<u>boh</u>*	sink
le robinet	*luh rohbee<u>nay</u>*	faucet
la serviette	*lah sairvee<u>yet</u>*	towel
le miroir	*luh mee<u>rwar</u>*	mirror
les toilettes	*lay twa<u>let</u>*	toilet

le lit	*luh lee*	bed
le lit d'appoint	*luh lee dap<u>wa-n</u>*	extra bed
la couverture	*lah coovair<u>toor</u>*	blanket
l'oreiller	*loray<u>yeh</u>*	pillow
le matelas	*luh mat<u>lah</u>*	mattress

Est-ce que vous avez une chambre libre ?
Eskuh vooza<u>vay</u> oon sho-mbr <u>leebr</u> ?
Do you have a room?

Pour une personne ou pour deux personnes ?
Poor oon pair<u>son</u> oow poor duh pair<u>son</u> ?
For one or two people?

Avec deux lits ou avec un grand lit ?
Ahvec <u>duh</u> <u>lee</u> oow ahvec <u>a-n</u> <u>gro-n</u> <u>lee</u> ?
With two beds or with one large bed?

Avec deux lits, svp.
Ahvec duh <u>lee</u>, seel voo <u>play</u>.
With two beds, please.

C'est combien ?
Say coh-mbee<u>ye-n</u> ?
How much is it?

Je reste trois nuits.
Jze <u>rest</u> trwa <u>nwee</u>.
I'm staying three nights.

C'est avec douche ?
Setahvec <u>doosh</u> ?
Does it have a shower?

70

EST-CE QUE VOUS AVEZ UNE CHAMBRE LIBRE ?

Est-ce que le petit déjeuner est compris ?
Eskuh luh puh<u>tee</u> dayjzu<u>nay</u> eh coh-m<u>pree</u> ?
Is breakfast included?

Camping

le camping	*luh co-m<u>peeng</u>*	campsite
la caravane	*lah cahrah<u>vahn</u>*	trailer
la tente	*lah to-nt*	tent
le sac de couchage	*luh sac duh coo<u>shajz</u>*	sleeping bag
l'eau potable	*loh poh<u>tahb</u>l*	drinking water
louer	*loo<u>way</u>*	rental

71

Est-ce qu'il y a une place pour une tente ?
Eskilleeyah oon plahce poor oon to-nt ?
Is there room for the tent?

Où sont les lavabos / les poubelles / les prises ?
Oow soh-n lay lahvahboh / lay poobell / lay preez ?
Where are the sinks / the garbage cans / the outlets?

Types of Lodging

Aside from hotel rooms, there are other lodging options of quality open to you in France. The **gîtes ruraux** network of rural farmhouses and country residences for rent is an excellent and inexpensive way to lodge. **Chambres d'hôtes** are rooms you can let in private houses, much like the Anglo-Saxon Bed and Breakfast. An inn, or **auberge,** offers rooms and either full board (**pension complète**) or half-board (**demi-pension**). Youth hostels are **auberges de jeunesse**.

Money, Mail and Phone Calls

Bank

la banque	*lah bo-nk*	bank
les espèces	*layzespess*	cash
encaisser	*o-nkessay*	to cash
l'argent	*larjzo-n*	money
le billet	*luh beeyay*	bank notes
la caisse	*lah kess*	cashier
la monnaie	*lah monnay*	change
la pièce	*lah peeyess*	coin
le guichet	*luh geeshay*	teller
le chèque	*luh shek*	check
changer	*sho-njzay*	change
signer	*see-nyay*	endorse/sign

la signature	*lah seenyah<u>toor</u>*	signature
le change	*luh sho-njz*	exchange
payer	*pay<u>yey</u>*	to pay
la carte de crédit	<u>*cahrt*</u> *duh cray<u>dee</u>*	credit card
la carte bleue (CB)	*cahrtuh <u>bluh</u>*	VISA/Mastercard
le distributeur /	*luh distreeboo<u>tuhr</u>*	ATM teller
guichet	*gee<u>shay</u>*	
automatique	*ohtohmah<u>teek</u>*	

Je voudrais changer vingt dollars.
Jze voo<u>dray</u> sho-n<u>jzay</u> va-n doh<u>laar</u>.
I would like to change $20 US.

Je voudrais encaisser ce chèque.
Jze voo<u>dray</u> o-nkes<u>say</u> suh <u>shek</u>.
I would like to cash this check.

Pas de monnaie, s'il vous plaît.
Pah duh mon<u>nay</u>, seel voo <u>play</u>.
No small change, please.

The Post Office

French mailboxes are hard to miss; they're bright yellow. You can always find one outside a **Café-Tabac**, where tobacco products as well as postage stamps and telephone cards are sold.

envoyer	*o-nvoy<u>yey</u>*	send
l'adresse	*lah<u>dress</u>*	address
la lettre	*lah letr*	letter
la boîte aux lettres	*lah bwaht oh <u>letr</u>*	mailbox
le timbre	*luh ta-mbr*	stamp
le facteur	*luh fak<u>tuhr</u>*	letter carrier
l'enveloppe	*lo-nvel<u>opp</u>*	envelope
le destinataire	*luh desteenah<u>tair</u>*	receiver
le tarif	*luh tah<u>reef</u>*	rates

le poids	*luh pwa*	weight
par avion	*parraveey<u>oh-n</u>*	air mail
le colis	*luh coh<u>lee</u>*	package
le bureau de poste	*luh boor<u>oh</u> duh <u>post</u>*	post office
la carte postale	*lah cahrt post<u>ahl</u>*	postcard

Quel est le tarif des lettres pour les États-Unis / l'Australie / le Canada ?
Kellay luh tah<u>reef</u> deh <u>letr</u> poor layzaytahzoo<u>nee</u> / lostrah<u>lee</u> / luh cahnah<u>dah</u> ?
What is the postage for a letter to the United States / Australia / Canada?

Quatre timbres à trois francs, sil vous plaît.
<u>Catr</u> <u>ta-mbr</u> ah trwa fro-n, seel voo <u>play</u>.
Four three-franc stamps, please.

Telephoning

Since the privatization and deregulation of the state telephone company, France Telecom, there are many telephoning options available to travelers and residents. One thing you'll need for sure is a **Télécarte** for making local and long-distance calls from public telephone booths called **cabines.** These cards can be purchased at all post offices, **tabacs,** and métro tellers.

Il y a un téléphone près d'ici ?
Illee<u>yah</u> a-n telay<u>phone</u> pray dees<u>see</u> ?
Is there a telephone nearby?

Où est le téléphone, s'il vous plaît ?
Oow ay luh telay<u>phone</u>, seel voo <u>play</u> ?
Where is the telephone, please?

Est-ce que je peux téléphoner ?
Eskuh jze <u>puh</u> telayphon<u>ay</u> ?
Can I make a telephone call?

Allô, qui est à l'appareil ?
Alloh, kee etah lapahrray ?
Hello, who's calling please?

Pardon, je me suis trompé de numéro.
Pardoh-n, jze muh swee troh-npay duh noomairoh.
Pardon me, I dialed a wrong number.

le coup de téléphone	*luh coo duh telayphone*	phone call
passer un coup de fil	*pahsay a-n coo duh feel*	make a call
téléphoner	*telephonay*	to telephone
décrocher	*dehcroshay*	to pick up
accrocher	*rahcroshay*	to hang up
l'indicatif	*la-ndicateef*	country code
le numéro de téléphone	*luh noomairoh duh telayphone*	telephone number
la tonalité	*lah tonaleetay*	dial tone
le répondeur	*luh rehpoh-nduhr*	answering machine
l'annuaire	*lahnnuair*	telephone book
la cabine publique	*lah cabeen poohbleek*	telephone booth
occupé	*ohquepay*	busy
Ne coupez pas !	*nuh coopay pah !*	Don't hang up!
Ne quittez pas !	*nuh keetay pah !*	Hang on!

Note: to call France from **your** country dial 00 33 and then the regional number (Paris is 1) followed by eight digits. To call the US and Canada from France dial 00 1 followed by the area code and the number. For the UK dial 00 44 followed by the area code and the number.

The Police

Où est le commissariat de police ?
Ooway luh comeesahreeyah duh poleess ?
Where is the police station?

On m'a volé...	**J'ai perdu...**
Oh-n mah vohlay ...	*Jzay pairdoo...*
My... has been stolen.	I lost ....

... mon appareil photo.	*moh-nahpahray foto*	... my camera...
... mes bagages.	*may bahgajz*	...my suitcase...
... mon portefeuille.	*moh-n portuhfoy*	...my wallet.
... mon sac à main.	*moh-n sackahma-n*	... handbag.
... mes papiers.	*may pahpyey*	... my passport...

faire une déclaration	*fare oon dehclahrahseeyoh-n*	to make a declaration
l'accident	*laxeedo-n*	accident
la police	*lah poleess*	police
l'agent de police	*lahjzo-n duh poleess*	policeman/woman
le flic (Slang)	*luh flick*	cop
le voleur /	*luh vohluhr /*	thief
la voleuse	*lah vohluhz*	
la prison	*lah preezoh-n*	prison
l'argent	*lahrjzo-n*	money
la clé de voiture	*lah clay duh vwatur*	car keys
la montre	*lah moh-ntr*	watch
la drogue	*lah drohg*	drugs

Au voleur !	*Oh vohlur !*	Stop that thief!
Au secours !	*Oh saycoor !*	Help!

Vos papiers, s'il vous plaît !
Vo papeeyeh, seel voo play !
Your papers (passport), please.

la douane	lah dwann	customs
le passeport	luh pahsepor	passport
la carte d'identité	lah cahrt deedo-nteetay	identity card
le visa	luh visah	visa
le nom	luh noh-n	last name
le prénom	luh praynoh-n	first name
l'adresse	ladress	address
la date / le lieu de naissance	lah daht / luh leeyuh duh naysso-ns	date of birth / place of birth
l'arrivée / l'entrée	larreevay / lo-ntray	arrival / entry
le départ / la sortie	luh daypahr / lah sortee	departure / exit
la durée du séjour	lah duray doo sayjzoor	length of stay
la nationalité	lah nahseeyonaleetay	nationality
la validité	lah valideetay	expiration date

Shopping

acheter	ahsh(e)tay	to buy
vendre	vo-ndr	to sell
le prix	luh pree	price
l'argent	larjzo-n	money
la monnaie	lah monnay	pocket change
le billet	luh beeyeh	paper money
cher	shair	expensive
trop cher	troh shair	too expensive
bon marché	boh-n marshay	cheap
le marché	luh marshay	market
le magasin	luh mahgahza-n	store
le propriétaire	luh prohpreeyetair	owner
la réduction	lah raydookseeyoh-n	discount
les soldes	lay sold	sale
grand choix	gro-n shwah	large selection
les heures d'ouverture	layzuhr doovairtoor	store hours
la qualité	lha kahleetay	quality

Où est-ce que je peux acheter un plan de la ville ?
Oow eskuh jze puh ahsh(e)tay a-n plo-n duh lah veel ?
Where can I buy a city map?

Vous avez des journaux étrangers ?
Voozahvay day jzoornoh etro-njzay ?
Do you have foreign newspapers?

Je voudrais un dictionnaire / un guide touristique.
Jze voodray a-n dicseeyonair / a-n geed turisteek.
I would like a dictionary / a travel guide.

Ça coûte combien ?   **Combien ça coûte ?**
Sah coot coh-nbeeye-n ?   *Coh-nbeeye-n sah coot ?*
                How much does it cost?

Je peux payer par chèque ?
Jze puh payyey pahr shek ?
Can I pay by check?

Est-ce que vous acceptez les cartes de crédit ?
Eskuh voozakceptay lay cahrt duh credee ?
Do you accept credit cards?

Most stores in France stay open to 7 p.m. (19h) but many close for lunch between noon and 2 p.m. (14h). Offices are closed on Saturdays but stores are usually open, however, many are closed on Mondays.

JE PEUX PAYER PAR CHÈQUE ?

Stores and Shops

la pharmacie	*lah pharma<u>cee</u>*	pharmacy
la boulangerie	*lah boolo-njzuh<u>ree</u>*	bread store
la librairie	*lah leebrai<u>ree</u>*	bookstore
livres d'occasion	*leavr dohcahsee<u>yoh-n</u>*	used books
le salon de coiffure	*luh sahloh-n duh kwa<u>foor</u>*	beauty parlor
le grand magasin	*luh gro-n mahgah<u>za-n</u>*	department store
la pâtisserie	*lah pahteesse<u>ree</u>*	bakery
l'épicerie	*lepeesse<u>ree</u>*	grocery store
la boucherie	*lah booshe<u>ree</u>*	butcher shop
la crèmerie	*lah craym(e)<u>ree</u>*	dairy/cheese shop
le pressing	*luh pres<u>sing</u>*	dry cleaner
la papeterie	*lah papaite<u>ree</u>*	stationery store
le cordonnier	*luh cordon<u>yey</u>*	shoemaker

le libre-service	*luh leebr sairveess*	self-serve
le supermarché	*luh soopairmarshay*	supermarket
la confiserie	*lah coh-nfeeseree*	candy store
le bureau de tabac	*luh booroh duh tahbah*	tobacco shop
la brocante	*lah broco-nt*	antique shop

Groceries

VIANDE	*veeyo-nd*	MEAT
... de bœuf	*duh buff*	beef
... de mouton	*duh mootho-n*	lamb
... de porc	*duh pohr*	porc
... de veau	*duh voh*	veal
la volaille	*lah vohlie*	poultry
le poulet	*luh poolay*	chicken
le canard	*luh cahnahr*	duck
la dinde	*lah da-nd*	turkey
le foie	*luh fwa*	liver
les tripes	*lay treep*	tripe
la cervelle	*lah sairvell*	brain
la charcuterie	*lah sharcooteree*	cold cuts
le jambon	*luh jzo-nboh-n*	ham
le saucisson	*luh sawseessoh-n*	sausage

FRUITS	*frwee*	FRUIT
l'abricot	*labreecoh*	abricot
le cassis	*luh cahseess*	black currant
la cerise	*lah sereez*	cherry
le citron	*luh seetroh-n*	lemon
la fraise	*lah frez*	strawberry
la framboise	*lah fro-mbwaz*	raspberry
la mûre	*lah moor*	blackberry
l'orange	*loro-njz*	orange
la pêche	*lah pesh*	peach
la poire	*lah pwar*	pear
la pomme	*lah pum*	apple
la prune	*lah proon*	plum
le raisin	*luh rayza-n*	grape

LÉGUMES	laygoom	VEGETABLES
l'ail	lie	garlic
l'artichaut	lahrteeshoh	artichoke
l'avocat	lahvocah	avocado
le chou-fleur	luh shoe fluhr	cauliflower
le concombre	luh coh-ncoh-mbr	cucumber
les épinards	layzepeenahr	spinach
les haricots	layzareecoh	beans
les herbes	layzairb	herbs
l'oignon	lonyoh-n	onion
les petits pois	lay petee pwah	peas
le poireau	luh pwaroh	leek
la pomme de terre	lah pum duh tair	potato
la carotte	lah cahrott	carrot

FRUITS DE MER	frwee duh mair	SEAFOOD
les crevettes	lay crevet	shrimp
les huîtres	layzwheatr	oysters
les moules	lay mool	mussels

POISSONS	pwassoh-n	FISH
le cabillaud	luh cahbeeyoh	cod
lae saumon	lah sohmoh-n	salmon
la truite	la trweet	trout

BOISSONS	bwassoh-n	DRINKS
l'eau	loh	water
le jus d'orange	luh jzoo doro-njz	orange juice
le vin	luh va-n	wine
la bière	lah beeyair	beer
le lait	luh lay	milk
le café	luh cahfay	coffee
le thé	luh tay	tea
l'infusion	la-nfooseeyoh-n	herbal tea

PRODUITS LAITIERS	*prodwee layteeyeh*	DAIRY
le beurre	*luh buhr*	butter
le fromage	*luh frohmajz*	cheese
le fromage blanc	*luh frohmajz blo-n*	cream cheese
le yaourt	*luh yahoort*	yogurt
la crème	*lah crem*	cream
l'œuf / les œufs	*luff / layzuh*	egg/eggs
la glace	*lah glahs*	ice cream

AUTRES		OTHER
le riz	*luh ree*	rice
les pâtes / les nouilles	*lay paht / lay nooy*	noodles
les céréales	*luh saireyal*	cereals
le miel	*luh meeyel*	honey
le sucre	*luh soocr*	sugar
les noix	*lay nwah*	nuts

Donnez-moi un kilo d'oranges, s'il vous plaît.
Donnay mwa a-n keeloh doro-njz, seel voo play.
I'll have a kilo of oranges, please.

Un beau morceau de fromage, s'il vous plaît.
A-n boh morsoh duh fro-mahjz, seel voo play.
I'll have a good size piece of cheese, please.

Il s'appelle comment ?	**Camembert.**
Ill sahpell kommo-n ?	*Cahmo-nbair.*
What's it called?	Camembert.

Smoking

If you are not a smoker, and chances are you're not, be prepared to be bothered by smoke and smokers in France. There is relatively little consciousness on the subject, and non-smokers' rights are far from protected. Your intolerance will not be appreciated. Legally, all cafés and restaurants must have places designated as **non-fumeur**, but this is not always applied, and the tables in that section are often the least scenic spots in the establishment. Tobacco sales are a huge source of revenue for the French state, which maintains a monopoly on these heavily-taxed products, which explains a lot.

les cigarettes	*lay cigah<u>ret</u>*	cigarettes
le cendrier	*luh so-ndree<u>yey</u>*	ashtray
le briquet	*luh bree<u>kay</u>*	lighter
la boîte d'allumettes	*lah bwaht dahloo<u>met</u>*	box of matches
fumeur	*foo<u>muhr</u>*	smoker
non fumeur	*noh-n foo<u>muhr</u>*	non-smoker
interdit de fumer	*a-ntair<u>dee</u> duh foo<u>may</u>*	No Smoking

Excusez-moi, est-ce que ça vous dérange si je fume ?
Exkoosay <u>mwa</u>, eskuh sah voo d<u>ero-njz</u> see jze <u>foom</u> ?
Excuse me, does it bother you if I smoke?

Excusez-moi, votre cigarette me dérange.
Exkoosay <u>mwa</u>, vohtr ciga<u>ret</u> muh d<u>ero-njz</u>.
Excuse me, your cigarette bothers me.

Eating and Drinking

As you may have already gathered, the French give a lot of importance to food and drink. Much of the social life and commercial life in France revolves around the table.

As a general rule, despite the apparent contradiction, keep in mind that anything one does to increase the pleasure and enjoyment of a meal is permissible.

If you don't drink wine and coffee, plan to be either miserable or ostracized. Don't order a cola with your meal but do order oysters, for goodness' sake! Eating in France for Anglo-Saxons in any case should be a mind (and belly) expanding experience.

Having said that, be warned: it is easy to eat very mediocre food and pay high prices in Paris today. Ask friends for recommendations. And stay away from the tourist traps. The menu is called **la carte** and the French word **menu** means the "fixed menu:" appetizer, main dish, dessert, wine and coffee, which is often a decent deal.

Tap water is served in bottles or carafes, but you have to ask for it. You'll never find ice cubes, so forget about it.

A word on tipping: service is almost always included in the prices on the menu, so don't simply add on 15%. What most people do is leave after a meal an extra five or ten francs in the little dish as a sign of satisfaction.

Une table pour deux personnes, s'il vous plaît.
Oon tahbl poor duh pair_son_, seel voo _play_.
A table for two, please.

La carte, s'il vous plaît.
Lah _cahrt_, seel voo _play_.
The menu, please.

Qu'est-ce qu'il y a comme plat du jour ?
Keskilleeyah cum _plah_ doo _jzoor_ ?
What's today's specialty?

Qu'est-ce que vous conseillez ?
Keskuh voo coh-nsay_yey_ ?
What do you recommend?

Je prends le menu à 89 francs.
Jze pro-n luh me_noo_ ah _cahtr_ _va-n_ _nuff_ _fro-n_.
I'll have the 89 francs menu.

Qu'est-ce que vous prenez comme boisson ?
Keskuh voo pre_nay_ cum bwas_soh-n_ ?
What would you like to drink?

QU'EST-CE QUE VOUS CONSEILLEZ ?

Une bouteille de vin blanc et une carafe d'eau, s'il vous plaît.
Oon boo<u>tay</u> duh va-n blo-n eh oon cah<u>raf</u> doh, seel voo <u>play</u>.
A bottle of white wine and a glass of water, please.

Et comme dessert ?
Eh cum days<u>sair</u> ?
And for dessert?

Pas de dessert, merci.
Pah duh days<u>sair</u>, mair<u>see</u>.
No dessert for me, thanks.

Je voudrais une glace / une crème caramel.
Jze voo<u>dray</u> oon glahs / oon krem cahrah<u>mell</u>.
I would like some ice cream / a caramel pudding.

L'addition, s'il vous plaît.
Ladeesee<u>yoh-n</u>, seel voo <u>play</u>.
The bill, please.

le repas	*luh ruhpah*	meal
le petit déjeuner	*luh petee dehjzenay*	breakfast
le déjeuner	*luh dehjzenay*	lunch
le dîner	*luh deenay*	dinner
le plat du jour	*luh plah doo jzoor*	daily special
le menu	*luh menoo*	menu
l'apéritif	*lapairiteef*	cocktail
les entrées	*layzo-ntray*	appetizers
la salade	*lah sahlahd*	salad
les fruits de mer	*lay frwee duh mair*	seafood
le pâté	*luh pahtay*	paté
la soupe	*lah soop*	soup
le potage	*luh powtajz*	soup
le plat	*luh plah*	dish
les légumes	*lay laygoom*	vegetables
végétarien	*vehjzehtahreeye-n*	vegetarian
le poisson	*luh pwassoh-n*	fish
la viande	*lah veeyo-nd*	meat
l'escalope	*lescalup*	(veal) cutlet
la brochette	*lah broshet*	skewer
le bifteck	*luh biftek*	steak
la sauce	*lah sauce*	sauce
le fromage	*luh frohmajz*	cheese
le dessert	*luh dayssair*	dessert
les fruits	*luh frwee*	fruit
la glace	*lah glahs*	ice cream
le gâteau	*luh gahtoh*	cake
la tarte	*lah tahrt*	pie
le café	*luh cahfay*	coffee
café au lait	*cahfay oh lay*	coffee with milk
café noir	*cahfay nwar*	black coffee
la tasse	*lah tahs*	cup

le digestif	*luh deegesteef*	after-dinner drink
la boisson	*lah bwassoh-n*	drinks
l'eau	*loh*	water
la bière	*lah beeyair*	beer
le vin	*luh va-n*	wine
le verre	*luh vair*	glass
la carafe	*lah cahraff*	carafe/pitcher
la table	*lah tahbl*	table
la chaise	*lah shez*	chair
le couvert	*luh coovair*	cutlery
le couteau	*luh cootoh*	knife
la fourchette	*lah foorshet*	fork
la cuillère	*lah kweeyair*	spoon
l'assiette	*lahseeyet*	plate
le poivre	*luh pwahvr*	pepper
le sel	*luh sel*	salt
l'huile	*lwheel*	oil
le vinaigre	*luh veenegr*	vinegar
la moutarde	*lah mootahrd*	mustard
le pain	*luh pa-n*	bread
le régime	*luh rayjzeem*	diet
la faim	*lah fa-n*	hunger
la soif	*lah swaf*	thirst
boire	*bwar*	to drink
le goût	*luh goo*	taste
gras	*grah*	fat
maigre	*megr*	lean
frais	*fray*	fresh
gratiné	*grahteenay*	broiled
cru	*croo*	raw
frit	*free*	fried
rôti	*rohtee*	roasted
farci	*farsee*	stuffed

Bon appétit !   *Bonahpeht<u>ee</u>*   Enjoy your meal!

The regional diversity of French cuisine is enticing. Burgundy, Alsace, Bretagne, Savoie, they all offer their own delicacies. Indulge.

In France, like in all contemporary societies, you'll find numerous restaurants specializing in foreign cuisine. For reasons related to France's colonial past, North African restaurants are plentiful. If you're curious and you have the time, it'd be well worth the experience stopping in at a little Algerian or Tunisian restaurant for a **couscous.** If you have to ask what's that, all the more reason to just do it. Morrocan food is particularly colorful and tasty and is considered one of the best cuisines in the world.

Where to Eat and Drink

café	coffee shop, café
salon de thé	tea room
bistrot	bistro, restaurant
brasserie	brasserie, restaurant
restaurant	restaurant
bar-tabac	bar and tobacco shop
libre-service	cafeteria
bar américain	standup bar

This may seem strange, but at **cafés** the prices of what you drink vary depending on where you're standing or sitting. The most expensive spots are the outside sidewalk **café** tables. The least expensive way to drink is to stand at the zinc bar. Night tariffs kick in after 8 p.m.

Une pression, s'il vous plaît.
Oon press<u>ioh-n</u>, seel voo <u>play</u>.
A draft beer, please.

Un demi, s'il vous plaît.
A-n de<u>mee</u>, seel voo <u>play</u>.
A beer, please.

Un verre / un ballon de rouge, s'il vous plaît.
A-n vair / a-n bahloh-n duh roozj, seel voo play.
A glass of red wine, please.

Un panaché, s'il vous plaît.
A-n pahnahshay, seel voo play.
A shandy (beer mixed with lemonade), please.

Un express, s'il vous plaît.
A-nexpress, seel voo play.
A coffee, please.

Un petit crème, s'il vous plaît.
A-n petee crem, seel voo play.
A small coffee with cream, please.

In Town

le séjour	*luh sayjzoor*	stay, visit
les vacances	*lay vaco-ns*	vacation / holiday
l'arrondissement	*larroh-ndiss(e)mo-n*	city district
Huitième	*wheateeyem*	8th district
Onzième, etc.	*ownzeeyem*	11th district
l'avenue	*lahvenoo*	avenue
la banlieue	*lah bo-nlyuh*	suburb
la capitale	*lah cahpeetahl*	capital
le carnet (de tickets)	*luh cahrnay duh teekay*	booklet of tickets
le centre-ville	*luh so-ntr veel*	city center
la cité universitaire	*lah ceetay ooneevairseetair*	university campus
la gare	*lah gahr*	train station
le gratte-ciel	*luh graht seeyel*	skyscraper
le métro	*luh mehtroh*	subway
le périphérique	*luh paireefaireek*	beltway
le piéton	*luh peeyeytoh-n*	pedestrian

la place	*lah plahs*	square
le plan de la ville	*luh plo-n duh lah veel*	city map
la pollution	*lah pohloosseyoh-n*	pollution
le quartier	*luh carteeyey*	neighborhood
la rue	*la roo*	street
l'office du tourisme	*loffeece doo tooreesmuh*	tourist office
le terminus	*luh tairmeenoos*	terminus
le trottoir	*luh trottwar*	sidewalk
l'usine	*loozeen*	factory
le village	*luh veelahjz*	town
la ville	*lah veel*	city
le bois	*luh bwa*	woods
la campagne	*lah co-npanye*	countryside
la cave	*lah cahv*	cellar
le cimetière	*luh cimeteeyair*	cemetery
la cour	*lah coor*	courtyard
l'église	*legleez*	church
les environs	*layzo-nveeroh-n*	environs
la fontaine	*lah foh-ntenn*	fountain
la forêt	*lah foray*	forest
l'hôtel de ville	*lohtel duh veel*	city hall
le marché	*luh marshay*	market
le marché aux puces	*luh marshay oh pooce*	flea market
la montagne	*lah moh-ntanye*	mountain
le musée	*luh moohzay*	museum
le parc	*luh pahrk*	park
le paysage	*luh payzahjz*	landscape
le pont	*luh poh-n*	bridge
la vallée	*lah valay*	valley
bronzer	*broh-nzay*	to tan
nager	*nahjzay*	to swim
faire de la plongée	*fair duh lah ploh-njzay*	to dive
faire de la voile	*fair duh lah vwahl*	to sail
la planche à voile	*lah plo-nsh ah vwahl*	windsurfing (board)

la côte	*lah coat*	coast
le fleuve	*luh fluv*	river
la mer	*lah mair*	sea
la plage	*lah plahjz*	beach
la rivière	*lah riveeyair*	river (small)
l'auberge	*lohbairjz*	inn
la caravane	*lah kahrah_vahn_*	camping car
la station de sports d'hiver	*lah stahseeyoh-n duh spor deevair*	winter sports location

Est-ce qu'on peut visiter... ?
Eskoh-n puh visitay... ?
Can I visit...?

Où est l'office de tourisme, s'il vous plaît ?
Oowway lofeess duh toureesm, seel voo play ?
Where is the tourist office, please?

Est-ce qu'il y a une visite guidée ?
Eskilleeyah oon viseet geeday ?
Is there a guided tour?

Quand est-ce que le musée est ouvert ?
Ko-nteskuh luh moozay etoovair ?
When is the museum open?

Arts and Leisure

les loisirs	*lay lwazeer*	leisure
la séance	*lah sayo-ns*	showing
le spectacle	*luh spektakl*	show
le théâtre	*luh tayatr*	theater
le concert	*luh coh-nsair*	concert
le cinéma	*luh seenayma*	cinema
le film	*luh feelm*	film

l'exposition	*lexpohzisseeyoh-n*	exhibition
sortir	*sorteer*	to go out (socially)
le pub	*luh puhb*	pub
la boîte	*lah bwaht*	disco
la boîte de nuit	*lah bwaht duh nwee*	nightclub
danser	*do-nsay*	to dance
le compact disc / CD	*luh coh-npact deesc / Sayday*	CD
la chaîne hi-fi	*lah shen hee fee*	stereo system
le sport	*luh spor*	sport
la piscine	*lah peesseen*	swimming pool

Note that in Paris the nightclubs and discos start late and continue until early morning.

The French go to the cinema a lot. And in most towns and cities you'll find a good selection of French and foreign films, which are often shown in **V.O. (version originale)**, meaning that they are in their original language with French subtitles. **V.F. (version française)** means that the film has been dubbed into French.

On va boire un pot ? Je t'invite.
Oh-n vah bwar a-n poh ? Jze ta-nveet.
Should we go for a drink? You're my guest.

D'accord.
Dakcor.
Okay!

Avec plaisir.
Ahvec playzeer.
With pleasure.

Est-ce qu'il y a un tarif réduit ?
Eskilleeyah a-n tahreef raydwee ?
Is there a reduced price?

Où peut-on danser ?
Oow puhtoh-n do-nsay ?
Where can we go dancing?

EST-CE QU'IL Y A UN TARIF RÉDUIT ?

Love and its Complications

amoureux	*ahmoor<u>ruh</u>*	in love
le coup de foudre	*luh coo duh <u>foodr</u>*	crush / lovestruck
le grand amour	*luh gro-nta<u>moor</u>*	passionate love affair
draguer / dragueur	*drah<u>gay</u> /drah<u>guhr</u>*	flirt / pick-up
être jaloux	*etr jzah<u>loo</u>*	to be jealous
tromper quelqu'un	*troh-m<u>pay</u> kel<u>ka-n</u>*	to cheat on someone
mettre à la porte	*metr ah lah <u>port</u>*	to kick out
l'ex	*lex*	ex, former
se faire des câlins	*suh fair day cah<u>la-n</u>*	caress
embrasser	*o-nbrah<u>say</u>*	to kiss

le baiser	*luh bai<u>zeh</u>*	kiss
la pillule	*lah pee<u>lool</u>*	the pill
le contraceptif	*luh coh-ntrassep<u>teef</u>*	contraceptive
le préservatif	*luh praysairva<u>teef</u>*	condom
le diaphragme	*luh deeah<u>frahgm</u>*	diaphram
le stérilet	*luh stairee<u>lay</u>*	IUD
les règles	*lay raygl*	period
les tampons	*lay to-n<u>poh-n</u>*	tampons
l'avortement	*lavorte<u>mo-n</u>*	abortion
la grossesse	*lah grohsess*	pregnancy
enceinte	*o-n<u>sa-nt</u>*	pregnant
le SIDA	*luh see<u>dah</u>*	AIDS

Toilets

| occupé | *ohcoo<u>pay</u>* | occupied |
| libre | *leebr* | free |

| Messieurs | *mes<u>syuh</u>* | men |
| Dames | *dahm* | women |

Où sont les toilettes, s'il vous plaît ?
Oow soh-n lay twa<u>let</u>, seel voo <u>play</u> ?
Where is the bathroom, please?

Il y a des W.C. publics ?
Illee<u>yah</u> day vays<u>say</u> poo<u>bleek</u> ?
Are there public toilets?

le papier hygiénique
luh papee<u>yay</u> heejzeeai<u>neek</u>
toilet paper

les serviettes hygiéniques
lay sairvee<u>yet</u> heejzeeai<u>neek</u>
sanitary napkins

Health and Illness

la pharmacie	*lah farmah<u>cee</u>*	pharmacy
l'hôpital	*lohpee<u>tall</u>*	hospital
le médecin	*luh meds<u>a-n</u>*	doctor
l'infirmière	*la-nfeermee<u>yair</u>*	nurse
le dentiste	*luh do-n<u>teest</u>*	dentist
la douleur	*lah doo<u>luhr</u>*	pain
malade	*mah<u>lahd</u>*	sick, ill
la maladie	*lah mahlah<u>dee</u>*	sickness, disease
l'examen	*lexzah<u>ma-n</u>*	examination, test
le diagnostic	*luh deeyagnos<u>teek</u>*	diagnosis
la radio	*lah rah<u>dyo</u>*	X-ray
le traitement	*luh tret<u>mo-n</u>*	treatment
le pansement	*luh po-ns<u>mo-n</u>*	bandage
la piqûre	*lah pee<u>cure</u>*	injection, shot
les comprimés	*lay coh-mpree<u>may</u>*	pills
vacciner	*vaksee<u>nay</u>*	to vaccinate
prescrire	*press<u>creer</u>*	to prescribe
l'ordonnance	*lordon<u>no-ns</u>*	prescription
contagieux	*coh-ntah<u>jziuh</u>*	contagious
faire mal	*fair <u>mahl</u>*	to hurt
blessé	*bles<u>say</u>*	injured
brûlé	*broo<u>lay</u>*	burned
cassé	*cahs<u>say</u>*	broken
respirer	*respee<u>ray</u>*	to breathe
tordu	*tor<u>doo</u>*	twisted
vomir	*voh<u>meer</u>*	to vomit
l'allergie	*lalair<u>jzee</u>*	allergy
la coupure	*lah coo<u>pure</u>*	cut
la fièvre	*lah fee<u>yevr</u>*	fever
la fracture	*lah frak<u>ture</u>*	fracture
l'infection	*la-nfeksee<u>yoh-n</u>*	infection
la nausée	*lah noh<u>zay</u>*	nausea
la plaie	*lah <u>play</u>*	wound
le plombage	*luh ploh-m<u>bajz</u>*	filling (dental)

le régime	*luh rayjzeem*	diet
le rhume	*luh rhoom*	a cold
la toux	*lah too*	cough

Parts of the Body

l'appendice	*lapa-ndeess*	appendix
le cerveau	*luh sairvoh*	brain
le cœur	*luh ker*	heart
l'estomac	*lestohmah*	stomach
le foie	*luh fwa*	liver
l'intestin	*la-ntesta-n*	intestines
le muscle	*luh mooscl*	muscle
l'os	*los*	bone
la peau	*lah poh*	skin
le poumon	*luh poomoh-n*	lung
le rein	*luh ra-n*	kidney
le sang	*luh so-n*	blood
la veine	*lah ven*	vein
la tête	*lah tet*	head
le visage	*luh veesajz*	face
l'œil / les yeux	*loy / layzyuh*	eye / eyes
la bouche	*lah boosh*	mouth
les dents	*lay do-n*	teeth
le nez	*luh nay*	nose
l'oreille	*lorey*	ear
la gorge	*lah gorjz*	throat
le cou	*luh coo*	neck
la nuque	*lah nuke*	nape
l'épaule	*lepohl*	shoulder
le bras	*luh brah*	arm
le coude	*luh cood*	elbow
le doigt	*luh dwa*	finger
la poitrine	*lah pwatreen*	breast
le ventre	*luh vo-ntr*	belly
le dos	*luh doh*	back

le pénis	*luh pe<u>nees</u>*	penis
le vagin	*luh vah<u>jza-n</u>*	vagina
la jambe	*lah jzo-mb*	leg
le genou	*luh jze<u>noo</u>*	knee
le pied	*luh pee<u>yay</u>*	foot
le talon	*luh tah<u>loh-n</u>*	heel

J'ai mal à la gorge / à la tête / aux dents.
Jzay mahl ah lah <u>gorjz</u> / ah lah <u>tet</u> / ooh <u>do-n</u>.
I have a sore throat / a headache / a toothache.

Ça fait mal.
Sah fay <u>mahl</u>.
That hurts.

J'ai besoin d'un médecin.
Jzay be<u>zwa-n</u> da-n med<u>sa-n</u>.
I need a doctor.

Appelez un médecin, s'il vous plaît.
Ahpe<u>lay</u> a-n med<u>sa-n</u>, seel voo <u>play</u>.
Call me a doctor, please.

J'AI MAL AUX DENTS.

97

Slang (*Argot*)

Slang in France is an integral part of daily, common language and thus attention must be given to the words that are not always taught in school or listed in language books. What's important here is that you are able to understand what you hear, and not so much your ability to use **argot** yourself. It takes time to master the right moment for the right word, so proceed with caution. Here are some of the slang words you'll hear regularly.

un machin	*a-n masha-n*	thing, thingamy
le truc	*luh trook*	thing, thingamy
le fric	*luh freek*	money/ dough
le boulot	*luh booloh*	work/ job
la bouffe	*lah boof*	food/chow, grub
bouffer	*boofay*	to eat/chow down
la bagnole	*lah bahnyol*	car
la nana	*lah nahnah*	girl/chick
le mec	*luh mec*	guy
le / la gosse / môme	*luh / lah gohs / mohm*	kid
piquer	*peekay*	to steal
branché	*bro-nshay*	"in"
la boum	*lah boom*	party
vachement	*vahshmo-n*	really
marrant	*mahro-n*	funny
cent balles	*so-n bahl*	hundred francs
la gueule	*lah guhl*	face/mug
gueuler	*guhlay*	to complain/bitch
s'engueuler	*so-nguhlay*	to bawl out
le bazar	*luh bahzahr*	mess
fabriquer	*fabreekay*	to make/do
la clope	*lah clup*	cigarette/butt
bosser	*bohssay*	to work
génial	*jzeneeyahl*	cool
chouette / super	*shwet / soopair*	super cool
connerie	*conneree*	stupid thing
le tube	*luh toob*	hit song

Just a quick note on **vachement** *(really)*. This adjective is used widely to give emphasis. Something that is **vachement loin** means it's *really far*. **Vachement joli** means *really pretty*. Got it? **Vachement chouette** is a double slang meaning really *cool!*

Commonly Heard Colloquial Expressions

Je suis crevé !	*Jze swee cre_vay_*	I'm dead tired.
Laisse tomber !	*Les_say_ toh-n_bay_*	Never mind!
Je craque !	*Jze crak*	I'm losing it!
Je m'en fous !	*Jze mo-n _foo_*	I don't give a damn!
C'est bidon !	*Say bee_doh-n_*	That's dumb!
J'en ai marre !	*Jzo-nay mar*	I'm fed up!

C'est rigolo / dingue / dément / sympa / extra / super.
*Say rigolo / da-ng / day_mo-n_ / sa-m_pah_ / ex_tra_ / soo_pair_*
It's funny / crazy / wacky / nice / great / super.

Interesting expressions beginning with **ça** (it's / that's):

ça va	*sah vah*	it's okay
ça suffit	*sah soo_fee_*	that's enough
ça nous dérange	*sah noo day_ro_-njz*	that's bothersome
ça me plaît	*sah muh _play_*	I like that
ça marche	*sah marsh*	that works
ça ne me regarde pas	*sah nuh muh re_gahrd_ pah*	that doesn't concern me
ça se peut	*sah suh puh*	that's possible
ça m'arrange	*sah mah_ro_-njz*	that helps me out
ça arrive	*sah ah_reev_*	it happens
ça t'intéresse ?	*sah ta-nte_ress_ ?*	does this interest you?

Getting Angry

Here are some words that you'll hear when people get angry or are experiencing a problem. Careful not to use these yourself unless you're completely sure of the meaning and the context.

Merde ! 💧	*maird*	shit
merdique 💧	*mair__deek__*	shitty
emmerder	*o-nmair__day__*	to bug someone
emmerdant	*o-nmair__do-n__*	a real pain in the ass
con 💧	*co__h-n__*	stupid, a drag
moche	*mohsh*	ugly
dégueulasse	*dayguh__lahss__*	disgusting
foutu 💧	*footoo*	fucked
putain 💧	*poo__ta-n__*	whore, damn it
bordel 💧	*bor__del__*	a mess
Espèce de con ! 💧	*es__pess__ duh coh-n*	asshole
Pauvre type !	*pohvr teep*	dumb ass!
Ç'est chiant !	*say shee__yo-n__*	that's shitty!
Fous le camp ! 💧	*foo luh co-n*	Fuck off!
Fiche-moi la paix !	*feesh mwa lah pay*	Leave me alone!
Arrête !	*ah__ret__*	Stop it!
Pas question !	*pah keste__yoh-n__*	No way!
Tu parles !	*too pahrl*	Yeah, right!
Tu rigoles !	*too ri__gohl__*	You're joking!
Tu déconnes !	*too day__cun__*	You're fucking up!
Ça suffit !	*sah soo__fee__*	That's enough!
Je vais te casser la gueule ! 💧	*Jze vay tuh cas__say__ lah guhl*	I'm going to kick your butt!
Ta gueule ! 💧	*tah guhl*	Shut the fuck up!

C'est nul / zéro / chiant / débile.
Say no__ol__ / zai__roh__ / shee__yo-n__ / day__beel__.
That sucks / It's a dud. / That sucks. / That's stupid.

Verlan (L'anver = l'envers)

Verlan is a form of backwards slang in French, like Pig Latin in English. The idea is to invert the syllables. A few examples:

une meuf (= une femme)	*oon muff*	a woman
un keum (= un mec)	*a-n kum*	a guy
le tromé (= le métro)	*luh tromay*	subway
le féca (= le café)	*luh fayca*	coffee

Franglais

A lot of English words have crept into daily French, although not always used exactly in the same way. Here are a few:

un rocker	*a-n rohkuhr*	rock 'n roller
le flirt	*luh flirt*	flirt
le meeting	*luh meeting*	meeting
le know-how	*luh no ow*	know how
le must	*luh muhst*	a must / to be in
D.J.	*dee dgee*	disc jockey
flipper	*fleepay*	to flip out
C'est cool !	*say kool*	cool

See what we mean!

Abbreviations

The French love to abbreviate. You'll see abbreviations for everything. Here are some of the most commonly heard:

ANPE	*ah-enn-peh-uh*	employment agency
RER	*air-uh-air*	commuter subway network
BD	*beh-deh*	comic strips
UE	*oo-uh*	European Union
HLM	*ahsh-ell-em*	state subsidized housing
SIDA	*seedah*	AIDS
K7	*kah-set*	cassette
SMIC	*smig*	minimum wage
SNCF	*ess-enn-say-eff*	railroad company
SVP	*ess-veh-peh*	please
TGV	*teh-jzeh-veh*	fast train
TVA	*teh-veh-ah*	sales tax
RATP	*air-ah-teh-peh*	Paris mass transit authority

Here, finally, are the most commonly encountered word expressions.

extra	**(-ordinaire)**	super
le ciné	**(-ma)**	the movies
la télé	**(-vision)**	TV
la manif	**(-estation)**	street demonstration
le métro	**(-politain)**	subway
le resto	**(-rant)**	restaurant
sympa	**(-thique)**	nice
le bac	**(-calauréat)**	high school degree
le prof	**(-esseur)**	professor
la photo	**(-graphie)**	photograph
le frigo	**(frigidaire)**	refrigerator
la pub	**(-licité)**	advertising
l'expo	**(-sition)**	exhibition
le petit-déj.	**(-euner)**	breakfast

If **French From the Word GO!** has motivated you to go further in French... Why not try Assimil's

New French with Ease

Let us help you move to a higher level of competency in French, improve your conversational skills, and build your vocabulary... intuitively of course. (See the next page.)

A Unique Principle: Intuitive Assimilation

How did you Learn to Speak your Own Language?
Chances are, you don't really know. **You listened to your parents, and bit by bit, began to understand them**. Then, once you had absorbed – or *assimilated* – **the meanings of the sounds, words** and word associations, you began to construct word groups and sentences yourself.

This is the **process that Assimil uses**. Naturally, we adapt our courses to take account of the fact that our readers are teenagers or adults who have already mastered their native language.

The Passive Phase
In the first phase, learners are simply getting acquainted with the new language, immersing themselves in it for about 20 to 30 minutes per day.

They listen to the text, then read and compare it with the English translation on the facing page. They repeat the sentences out loud in order to learn the prononciation, using the phonetic transcriptions provided in the book and the recordings.

During this phase, the **learning process is passive**. Learners do not try to form their own sentences, but simply **"soak up" the language**.

The Active Phase
After completing the first half of the book, the learners have acquired enough vocabulary and automatic reflexes to **begin creating and forming their own sentences**. This is the acquisitive phase of the learning process, which involves completing one "active" lesson and one "passive" lesson each day.

In the active phase, learners simply **cover the target-language text and reformulate it out loud** – and in writing, if desired – **using the translation text** on the facing page.

The active phase continues throughout the second half of the book. Thus, a course with 100 lessons will be assimilated in **about five months for the most common languages**.

The result is a firm grasp of the new language, acquired intuitively, which can be used and built upon without effort or hesitation.

Method Books

Lessons and exercises recorded on cassettes and CDs.
Perfect bound and illustrated.

Beginning Level:

Arabic with Ease
Dutch with Ease
New French with Ease
German with Ease
Hungarian with Ease
Italian with Ease
Spanish with Ease

Advanced Level:

Using French
Business French
Using German
Using Spanish

GLOSSARY

m	masculine	qqn (= quelqu'un)	someone
f	feminine	qqch (=quelque chose)	something
pl	plural		
*	irregular verb		

French-English

A

à	at, to
à peu près	about, more or less
abeille, f	bee
abréviation, f	abbreviation
absent	absent
absolument	absolutely
abus, m	abuse
accélérer	to accelerate
accepter	to accept
accès, m	access
accident, m	accident
accompagner	to accompany
achat, m	purchase
acheter	to buy
achever	to complete
acide	sour
activité, f	activity
addition, f	addition
administration, f	administration
admirer	to admire
adresse, f	address
aéroport, m	airport
affaire, f	business
affreux	frightful
âge, m	age

agence, f	agency
agent de police, m	police officer
agir	to act
agréable	nice
aider qqn	to help someone
aiguille, f	sharp
ail, m	garlic
ailleurs	elsewhere
aimable	friendly
aimer	to love
aimer bien	to like
air, m	air
aller*	to go
aller* chercher	to go get
allonger	to lengthen
allumer	to ignite
allumette, f	matches
altitude, f	altitude
ambassadeur, m	ambassador
améliorer	to improve
amer	bitter
ami/e	friend
amour, m	loved one
ampoule, f	bulb
amuser (s')	to have fun
an, m	year
animal, m	animal

année, f	year
annonce, f	advertisement
annuaire, m	directory
annuel	annual
appareil, m	apparatus, machine
apparemment	apparently
appartement, m	apartment
appeler	to call
appeler (s')	to call oneself
apprendre	to learn
approcher (s')	to approach
après	after, later
après-demain	the day after tomorrow
après-midi, m or f	afternoon
arbre, m	tree
argent	money
armoire, f	cupboard
arrêt, m	stop
arrêter	to stop
arrière (en)	behind
arrivée, f	arrival
arriver	to arrive
art, m	art
article	article
artiste, m + f	artist
ascenseur, m	elevator
asseoir* (s')	to sit oneself down
assez	enough
assiette, f	plate
assurance, f	insurance
assurer	to insure
atteindre*	to turn off
attendre	to wait
attentif	watchful
Attention !, f	Watch out!
attestation, f	statement
attester	to attest
attraper	to catch
au lieu de	instead of
au milieu de	in the midst of
au moins	at least
auberge, f	inn
aucun	none
au-dessous de	below
au-dessus de	above
augmenter	to increase
aujourd'hui	today
aussi	also
authentique	authentic
automatique	automatic
automne, m	autumn, fall
autorisé (à)	authorized (to)
autour de	around, about
autre	other, another
autrefois	formerly
autrement	otherwise
avant	before
avantage, m	advantage
avant-hier	the day before yesterday
avare	miserly
avec	with
avenir, m	future
avertir	to warn
aveugle	blind
avion, m	airplane
avocat, m	avocat
avoir*	to have
avoir* besoin de	to need
avoir* faim	to be hungry
avoir* froid	to be cold
avoir* l'air	to seem
avoir* l'intention	to intend

avoir* raison	to be right
avoir* soif	to be thirsty
avoir* tort	to be wrong

B

bagages, m pl.	luggage
bague, f	ring
baie, f	bay, berry
baigner (se)	to bathe, to swim
bain, m	bath
baiser, m	to kiss
bal, m	ball, dance
balance, f	scale
ballon, m	ball, balloon
banc, m	bench
banlieue, f	suburbs
banque, f	bank
bas	low (down)
bas (en)	below, downstairs
bateau, m	boat
bâtiment, m	building
bâton, m	stick
battre*	to beat
beau	handsome, nice
beaucoup	a lot
beau-frère, m	brother-in-law
beauté, f	beauty
bébé, m	baby
belge	Belgian
Belgique	Belgium
belle-sœur, f	sister-in-law
besoin, m	need
bête, adj	stupid
beurre, m	butter
bicyclette, f	bicycle
bien que	although
bientôt	soon

bienvenu(e)	welcome
bière, f	beer
bijou, m	jewel
billet, m	ticket
bistrot, m	restaurant
bizarre	strange
blague, f	joke
blanc	white
blessure, f	wound
bleu	blue
blond	blond
bœuf, m	beef
boire*	to drink
bois, m	wood
boisson, f	drink
boîte aux lettres, f	mailbox
boîte de nuit, f	nightclub
boîte, f	box
bon	good
bouche, f	mouth
boue, f	mud
bougie, f	candle
boulanger, m	baker
boulangerie, f	bakery
bouquet, m	bouquet
bouteille, f	bottle
bouton, m	button, pimple
bracelet, m	bracelet
branche, f	branch
bras, m	arm
briller	to shine
briquet, m	lighter
bronzer	to tan
brosse, f	brush
brouillard, m	fog
bruit, m	noise
brun	brown, dark
bruyant	noisy

bureau, m	desk, office
bus	bus
but, m	goal

C

cabane, f	cabin
cadeau, m	gift
café, m	coffee, coffee shop
cahier, m	notebook
calculer	calculate
calendrier, m	calendar
calme	calm
caméra, f	movie camera
camion, m	truck
camping, m	camp site
capable	able
capitale	capital
car, m	bus, coach
carrefour, m	intersection
carré	square
carte, f	card, menu
carte d'identité, f	identity card
carte géographique, f	map
carte postale, f	post card
cas d'urgence, m	emergency
casser	to break
casserole, f	pot
cathédrale, f	cathedral
cause, f	cause
causer	to cause
cave, f	cellar
célèbre	famous
célibataire	single
centre, m	center
certain	certain

cerveau, m	brain
chacun	each person
chaise, f	chair
chaleur, f	heat
chambre, f	room
champ, m	field
champignon, m	mushroom
chance, f	luck
change, m	change
changer	to change
chanson, f	song
chanter	to sing
chaque fois	each time
charger	to charge
chat, m	cat
château, m	chateau
chaud	hot
chauffage, m	heating
chauffer	driver
chaussette, f	sock
chaussure, f	shoe
chemin, m	path, way
chemise, f	shirt
chèque, m	check
cher	dear, expensive
chercher	to search
cheval, m	horse
cheveux, m pl.	hair
chien, m	dog
chiffre, m	figure, number
choisir	to chose
choix, m	choice
chose, f	thing
ciel, m	sky
cimetière, m	cemetery
cinéma, m	cinema
circonstance, f	circumstance
circulation, f	circulation
ciseaux, m pl.	scissors
clair	light

classe, f	class
clé, f	key
clou, m	nail
cœur, m	heart
coiffeur, m	hairdresser
coin, m	corner
colère, f	anger
collectionner	to collect
colline, f	hill
combien	how much
comestible	edible
commande, f	order
commander	to order
comme	like, as
comme ça	like that
comme si	as if
commencer	to begin
comment	how
comparaison, f	comparison
comparer	to compare
complètement	completely
composer	to compose
comprendre*	to understand
comprimé, m	tablet
compter	to count
concernant	concerning
concours, m	contest
condition, f	condition
conduire	to drive
confiance	confidence
confiance (avoir)	to trust
confirmer	to confirm
confiture, f	jam
confondre	to confuse
confortable	comfortable
congé, m	day-off
connaître*	to know (person or place)
connu	known

consentir*	to consent
considérable	considerable
consigne, f	deposit
consommer	to consume
construire*	to construct
content	content
contenu, m	contents
continuer	to continue
contraire, m	opposite
contrat, m	contract
contre	against
contrôleur, m	inspector
convaincre*	to convince
conversation	conversation
coq	rooster, cock
corde	cord
cordonnier	shoemaker
corps	body
correspondance	correspondence
côte, f	rib, slope, coast
côté, m	side
côté (à)	next to
coton, m	cotton
cou, m	neck
coudre*	to sew
couler	to flow
couleur, f	color
coup, m	strike, blow
coup de téléphone, m	phone call
couper	to cut
cour, f	court, yard
courant, m	current
courir*	to run
court	short
couteau, m	knife
coûter	to cost
coûteux	costly
coutume, f	custom
couverture, f	blanket

craindre*	to be afraid of	déjeuner	to have lunch
crainte, f	fear	demain	tomorrow
crayon, m	pencil	demande, f	request
crépuscule, m	twilight	demander	to request
crier	to shout	déménager	to move out
crime, m	crime	demi	half
croire	to believe	dent, f	tooth
cru	raw	dentiste, m	dentist
cuillère, f	spoon	départ, m	departure
cuir, m	leather	dépêcher (se)	to hurry
cuisine, f	kitchen	dépenser	to spend
cuit	cooked	dépenses, f	expenses
curieux	curious	depuis	since
		déranger	to bother
D		dernier, m	last
		dernière, f	last
d'abord	at first	derrière	behind
D'accord !	agreed, okay	désagréable	disagreeable
danger, m	danger	descendre	to go down
dangereux	dangerous	déshabiller (se)	to undress
dans	in	désir, m	desire
danse, f	dance	désirer	to desire
danser	to dance	désolé (être)	to be sorry
date, f	date	désordre, m	disorder
de	of, from	dessiner	to draw
de nouveau	again	détail, m	detail
début, m	beginning	détour, m	detour
décharger	to discharge, to unload	détruire*	to destroy
		deuxième	second
décider	to decide	devant	in front
décision, f	decision	développe-	development
déclarer	to declare	ment, m	
découvrir*	to discover	développer	to develop
déçu	disappointed	devenir*	to become
dedans	within	déviation, f	deviation
défaut, m	fault	devoir*	must
défendre	to defend	devoir, m	task, homework
dehors	outside	différence, f	difference
déjà	already	différent	different
déjeuner, m	lunch	difficile	difficult

difficulté, f	difficulty
dîner, m	to dine
dire*	to say, to tell
direct	direct
direction, f	direction
diriger (se)	to head for
disparaître*	to disappear
dispute, f	dispute
disque, m	record, disk
distinguer	to distinguish
distributeur automatique, m	ATM
diviser	to divide
doigt, m	finger
dommage !	pity!
dommage, m	damage
donc	therefore
donner	to give
dormir*	to sleep
dos, m	back
douane, f	customs
double	double
douche, f	shower
douleur, f	pain
doute, m	doubt
doux	soft, mild, sweet
douzaine, f	dozen
drap, m	sheet
droit	right, law
droite (à)	to the right
droits, m	rights
dur	hard
durée, f	duration
durer	to last

E

eau, f	water
échange, m	exchange
échanger	to exchange
éclair, m	flash
éclairer	to light up
école, f	school
écouter	to listen
écrire*	to write
écriture, f	writing
éducation, f	education
effet, m	effect
efficace	efficient
effort, m	effort
égal	equal
église, f	church
élections, f	elections
élève, m + f	pupil
éloigné	far-off
embrasser	to kiss
émission, f	show
empêcher	to prevent
employé, m	employee
employée, f	employee
employer	to employ
emprunter	to borrow
en	in, on
enceinte	pregnant
encore	more, still
endormir (s')	to fall asleep
endroit, m	place
enfant, m + f	child
enfin	finally
ennuyeux	boring
enseigner	to teach
ensemble	together
ensuite	then, next
entendre	to hear
entier	whole
entre	between
entrée, f	entry
entreprise, f	company, firm
entrer	to enter

entrez !	come in!
enveloppe, f	envelop
environ	about, around
environne-ment, m	environment
environs, m	surroundings
envoyer	to send
épais	thick
épargner	to save
épaule, f	shoulder
épeler	to spell
épingle, f	pin
époque	epoch
époque (à cette)	at the time
épuisé	worn out, out of stock
erreur, f	error
escalier, m	staircase
escargot, m	snail
espace, m	space
espèces, f	cash
espérer	to hope
esprit, m	spirit
essai, m	attempt
essayer	to attempt
essence, f	gasoline
est, m	east
estimer	to estimate
estomac, m	stomach
et	and
étang, m	pond
État, m	state
été, m	summer
éteindre*	to turn off
étendue, f	extent, area
étoffe, f	fabric
étoile, f	star
étrange	strange
étranger, m	foreigner
étranger/e	foreigner

être*	to be
être* ami(e)	to be friends
être* assis	to be seated
être* capable de	to be able to
être* couché	to be lying down
être* debout	to be standing
étroit	narrow
étudiant/e	student
événement, m	event
éviter	to avoid
exact	exact
exagéré	exaggerated
examiner	to examine
excellent	excellent
exception, f	exception
excursion, f	excursion
excuser	to excuse
exemple, m	example
exercer	to exercise
exiger	to insist
expérience, f	experience
expliquer	to explain
exposition, f	exhibition
expressément	deliberately
expression, f	expression
exprès	on purpose
extérieur (à l')	outside
externe	external
extraordinaire	extraordinary

F

face (en)	in front
fâcher (se)	to get angry
facile	easy
facteur, m	mailman (woman)
faible	feeble, weak

faiblesse, f	weakness	finalement	finally
faim, f	hunger	fixer	to fix
faire*	to do, to make	fleur, f	flower
faire* l'amour	to make love	fleurir*	to flower
faire* attention (à)	to pay attention (to)	fleuve, m	river
		foie, m	liver
faire* des courses	to go shopping	fois (une)	once
		fonctionnement	functioning
faire* des études	to study	fonctionner	to function
		force, f	strength, force
faire* la connaissance	to be introduced	forcer	to force
		forêt, f	forest
faire* la cuisine	to cook	fort	strong
		fou	crazy
faire* un effort	to make an effort	fourchette, f	fork
		fragile	fragile
fait, m	fact	frais	fresh
famille, f	family	frais, m	cost
fatigant	tiring	Français	French
fatigué (être)	to be tired	français	French
faute, f	fault	France, f	France
faux	fake, wrong	frapper	to strike
félicitations, f pl	congratulations	frère, m	brother
		frigidaire, m	refrigerator
féminin	feminine	froid	cold
femme, f	woman	fromage, m	cheese
fenêtre, f	window	frontière, f	border
ferme, f	farm	fruit, m	fruit
fermé	closed	fumée, f	smoke
fermer	to close	fumer	to smoke
fermer (à clé)	to lock	furieux	furious
feu, m	fire	futur	future
feuille, f	sheet, leaf		
fiche, f	form, card	**G**	
fièvre, f	fever		
fil, m	thread, wire	gagner	to win
filet, m	net	gai	cheerful
fille, f	girl, daughter	garçon, m	boy
fils, m	son	garder	to keep, to watch over
fin	end		

gare, f	station
garer (se)	to park
gauche (à)	on the left
général	general
genou, m	knee
gens, m	people
gentil/le	nice
glace, f	ice cream
gorge, f	throat
goût, m	taste
goutte, f	drop
gouverne- ment, m	government
grâce à	thanks to
grand	big
grand magasin, m	department store
grand-mère, f	grandmother
grand-père, m	grandfather
gras	fat
gratte-ciel, m	skyscraper
gratuit	free
grave	serious
grille, f	gate
gris	grey
gros	big, fat
groupe, m	group
guerre, f	war
guide, m	guide
guider	to guide

H

habiller (s')	to get dressed
habitant, m	inhabitant
habiter	to inhabit
habitude, f	habit
habituel	usual
habituer (s')	to get used to

haut	high
haut (en)	up
hebdomadaire	weekly
hésiter	to hesitate
heure, f	hour, time
heure (à l')	on time, hourly
heureux	happy
hier	yesterday
histoire, f	history, story
hiver, m	winter
homme, m	man
hôpital, m	hospital
horrible	horrible
hors de question	out of the question
hôtel, m	hotel
huile, f	oil
humide	damp, wet

I

ici	here
idée, f	idea
il y a	ago, there is, there are
île, f	island
illuminé	lit up
important	important
impossible	impossible
imprécis	imprecise
impression, f	impression
imprudent	imprudent
inattendu	unexpected
incendie, m	fire
incertain	uncertain
inconnu	unknown
incroyable	incredible
indécent	indecent
indispensable	indispensable

inévitable	inevitable	jour de fête, m	holiday
inflammable	flammable	journal, m	newspaper
information, f	information	jours (tous les)	everyday
injuste	unjust	juger	to judge
innocent	innocent	jupe, f	skirt
inquiéter (s')	to worry	jus, m	juice
insister sur	to insist upon	jusqu'à	until
insolent	insolent	jusqu'ici	up to here
insuffisant	insufficient	juste	just
insupportable	intolerable	justement	exactly
intelligent	intelligent		
intention, f	intention	**L**	
interdit	forbidden		
intéressant	interesting	là	here
intérieur (à l')	inside	là-bas	there
interprète,	interpreter	lac, m	lake
m + f		laid	ugly
interrompre	to interrupt	laine, f	wool
inutile	useless	laisser	to leave, to let
inventer	to invent	lait, m	milk
invitation, f	invitation	lampe de	flashlight,
inviter	to invite	poche, f	torch
itinéraire, m	itinerary	langue, f	language
		large	wide
J		laver	to wash
		laver (se)	to wash yourself
jamais	never	léger	light
jardin, m	garden	légumes, m	vegetables
jaune	yellow	lent	slow
jeter	to throw	lettre, f	letter
jeu de	playing cards	lever (se)	to get up
cartes, m		lèvre, f	lip
jeu, m	play	liberté, f	liberty
jeune	young	libre	free
joie, f	joy	lieu, m	place
joli	pretty	lièvre, m	hare
jouer	to play	ligne, f	line
jour, m	day	liquide	liquid, cash
jour (le)	daytime	lire*	to read

liste, f	list	malheur, m	misfortune
lit, m	bed	malheureuse-	unfortunately
litre, m	liter	ment	
livre, m	book	malicieux	malicious
livrer	to deliver	manger	to eat
logis, m	abode, home	manière, f	manner, way
loi, f	law	manque, m	lack of, shortage
loin	far	manquer	to lack, to be missing
loisirs, m	leisure		
long	long		
longtemps	a long time	manteau, m	coat
longueur, f	length	marchander	to bargain
louer	to rent	marchandise, f	merchandise
lourd	heavy	marché, m	market
loyer, m	rent	marcher	to walk
lumière, f	light	mari, m	husband
lune, f	moon	mariage, m	wedding
lunettes, f	glasses	marier (se)	to get married
		marteau, m	hammer

M

		masculin	masculine
machine, f	machine	matin (le)	morning (in the)
madame	Mrs.	mauvais	bad
mademoiselle	Miss	méchant	nasty
magasin, m	store	médecin, m	doctor
maigre	skinny	Méditerranée, f	Mediterranean
maillot de	bathing suit	méfiance, f	distrust
bain, m		meilleur	best
main, f	hand	même	even
maintenant	now	même (le)	the same
mais	but	même pas	not even
maison, f	house	mensonge, m	lie
mal à l'aise	uneasy	mensuel	monthly
malade	sick, ill	mer, f	sea
maladie, f	illness	merci	thank you
malchance, f	bad luck	mère, f	mother
malentendu, m	misunder-	mesure, f	measure
	standing	mesurer	to measure
malgré	despite	mètre, m	meter
		mettre*	to put, to place

meuble, m	furniture	moyen/ne	average
midi, m	noon	moyen, m	means
miel, m	honey	mur, m	wall
milieu, m	middle	mûr	ripe
mince	slim	musée, m	museum
minuit	midnight	musique, f	music
minute, f	minute		
miroir, m	mirror	**N**	
moderne	modern		
modifier	to modify	nager	to swim
mois, m	month	naissance, f	birth
mois (par)	monthly	nation, f	nation
moitié, f	half	nationalité, f	nationality
molester	to bother, to molest	nature, f	nature
		naturel	natural
moment, m	moment	nécessaire	necessary
monde, m	world	négliger	to neglect
monnaie, f	coins, money	neige, f	snow
monsieur	Mister	nettoyer	to clean
montagne, f	mountain	neuf	nine
montant, m	amount	neveu, m	nephew
monter	to go up	nez, m	nose
montre, f	watch	ni... ni	neither... nor
montrer	to show	nièce, f	niece
monument, m	monument	nier	to deny
morceau, m	piece	n'importe où	anywhere
mort	dead	n'importe quoi	anything
mort, f	death	né	born
mot, m	word	Noël	Christmas
moteur, m	motor	noir	black
moto, f	motorcycle	nom, m	name
mou	soft	nombre, m	number
mouche, f	fly	nombreux	numerous
mouchoir, m	handkerchief	non	no
mouillé	wet	nord, m	north
mourir*	to die	normal	normal
moustache, f	moustache	note, f	note
moustique, m	mosquito	nourriture, f	food
mouvement, m	movement	nouveau	new

nouvelle, f	news
nu	nude
nuage, m	cloud
nuisible	harmful
nuit, f	night
nulle part	nowhere
numéro, m	number

O

objet, m	object
obscurité, f	darkness
observer	to observe
occasion, f	occasion
occuper de (s')	to deal with, to take care of
occupé	occupied, busy
océan, m	ocean
odeur, f	smell
œil, m	eye
œuf, m	egg
œuvre, f	work
offenser	to offend
offre, f	offer
offrir*	to offer, to give for free
oiseau, m	bird
ombre, f	shadow
on	we
oncle, m	uncle
opéra, m	opera
opinion, f	opinion
opposé	opposed
orage, m	storm
ordre, m	order
ordures, f	garbage
oreille, f	ear
oreiller, m	pillowcase
os, m	bone

oser	to dare
ou	or
où	where
où (d')	from where
ou... ou	either... or
oublier	to forget
ouest, m	west
oui	yes
outil, m	tool
ouvert	open
ouvrier, m	worker
ouvrir*	to open

P

page, f	page
pain, m	bread
paix, f	peace
pâle	pale
panne	breakdown
pantalon, m	pants
papier à lettre, m	writing paper
papier, m	paper
Pâques	Easter
paquet, m	package
par cœur	by heart
par hasard	by chance
parapluie, m	umbrella
parc, m	park
parce que	because
pardon !	pardon!, excuse me!
pardonner	to excuse
pareil	same
parent	parent
parents, m	parents
paresse, f	laziness
paresseux	lazi

parfait	perfect	personnel	personal
parfois	sometimes	persuader	to persuade
parking, m	parking	peser	to weigh
parler	to speak, to talk	petit	small
parmi	among	petit déjeuner, m	breakfast
partager	to share		
partir*	to leave	petite-fille, f	granddaughter
partout	everywhere	petit-fils, m	grandson
pas	not	peu	little
pas cher	inexpensive	peuple, m	people
pas encore	not yet	peur, f	fear
passé	past	peut-être	maybe
passeport, m	passport	pharmacie, f	pharmacy
patience, f	patience	photo, f	photo
patron, m	boss, owner	phrase, f	sentence
pauvre	poor	pickpocket, m	pickpocket
payer	to pay	pièce, f	piece
payer en espèces	to pay in cash	pied, m	foot
		pied (à)	on foot
pays, m	country	pierre, f	stone
paysage, m	landscape	pilule, f	pill
paysan, m	farmer	piquer	to sting
peau, f	skin	piscine, f	swimmingpool
pêcher	to fish	place, f	place
pêcheur, m	fisherman	plafond, m	ceiling
peigne, m	comb	plage, f	beach
peindre*	paint, to	plaindre* (se)	to complain
peinture, f	painting	plainte, f	complain
pendant	during	plaire*	to please
penser	to think	plaisanterie, f	joke
perdre	to loose	plaisir, m	pleasure
père, m	father	plan, m	plan
périmé	expired	plante, f	plant
permanent	permanent	plat	flat
permettre*	to permit, to allow	plein	full
		pleurer	to cry
permis	license	pleuvoir*	to rain
permission, f	permission	plonger	to dive
personne	person	pluie, f	rain
personne, f	no one, nobody		

plus	plus, more	prénom, m	first name
plus ou moins	more or less	préparer	to prepare
plus tard	later	présent	present
plus tôt	earlier	présenter	to present
plutôt	more like, rather	presque	almost
pneu, m	tire	pressé	rushed
poche, f	pocket	prêter	to lend
poêle, m	pan	prétexte, m	pretext
poids, m	heavy	prêt	ready
poire, f	pear	preuve, f	proof
poisson, m	fish	prévenir* qqn	to warn, to notify
poitrine, f	breast		
poivre, m	pepper	printemps, m	spring
police, f	police	prison, f	prison
pomme, f	apple	privé	private
pomme de terre, f	potato	prix, m	price
		probable	probable
pont, m	bridge	prochain/e	next
porc, m	pig	prochainement	shortly
port, m	port	proche	near
porte, f	door	procurer	to procure
portefeuille, m	wallet	produit, m	product
porter	to carry	professeur, m	professor, teacher
posséder	to possess		
possible	possible	profession, f	profession
poste, f	post office	profond	deep
potable	drinkable	progrès, m	progress
poudre, f	powder	promener (se)	to stroll
pour	for	promettre*	to promise
pourboire, m	tip	prononcer	to pronounce
pour-cent, m	percent	prononciation, f	pronunciation
pourquoi ?	why?	proposer	to propose, to offer
pourri	rotten		
pousser	to grow	proposition, f	proposition
poussière, f	dust	propre	clean
pouvoir*	power	propriétaire, m	owner
pratique	practical	prospectus, m	prospectus
précaution, f	precaution	protection, f	protection
préférer	to prefer	protester	to protest
prendre*	to take	prouver	to prove

provisoirement	temporarily
prudent	prudent
public	public
publicité, f	advertisement
puer	to stink
puits, m	well
puisque	since, as
pur	pure

Q

quai, m	quai, bank
qualité, f	quality
quand	when
quantité, f	quantity
quart, m	quarter
quartier, m	neighborhood
que	that
quelque chose	something
quelques, pl	some
quelqu'un	someone
question, f	question
qui	who
quitter	to leave
quoi ?	what?
quotidien	daily

R

raccourci, m	short cut
raconter	to tell
radio, f	radio
raisin, m	grape
raison, f	reason
raisonnable	reasonable
randonnée, f	hike
rapide	fast
rappeler	to call back
rappeler (se)	to remember
rare	rare

rasoir, m	razor
ravissant	ravishing
réaliser	to achieve
réalité, f	reality
récemment	recently
réception, f	reception
recevoir*	to receive
recommander	to recommend
reconnaissant	grateful
reconnaître*	to acknowledge
réduction, f	reduction
réel	real
refuser	to refuse
regard, m	look
regarder	to look at
région, f	region
régler	to pay
regret, m	regret
regretter	to regret
reine, f	queen
remarquer	to notice
rembourser	to reimburse
remercier	to thank
remorquer	to tow
remplacer	to replace
remplir	to complete, to fill
rencontrer	to meet
rendez-vous, m	rendez-vous, appointment
rendre	to render
rendre possible	to make possible
rendre visite	to pay a visit
renseigne-ment, m	information
renseigner (se)	to inform oneself
renversé	knocked over
réparation, f	reparation

répartir	to divide up	rond	round
repas, m	meal	roue, f	wheel
répéter	to repeat	rouge	red
répondre	to answer	rue, f	street
réponse, f	answer	ruelle, f	lane
repos, m	rest		
reposer (se)	to rest, to relax	**S**	
représenta- tion, f	representation	sable, m	sand
réserve	reserve	sac, m	sack, bag
réserver	to reserve	sac à dos, m	backpack
résoudre*	to resolve	sac de couchage, m	sleeping bag
respecter	to respect	saigner	to bleed
respirer	to breathe	saisir	to seize, to grasp
responsable	responsible		
ressembler	to put together	saison	season
restant	remaining	salade, f	salad
reste, m	remains, left-overs	sale	dirty
		salé	salty
rester	to stay	saleté, f	dirt
résultat, m	result	salle, f	room, hall
retard, m	delay	salon de thé, m	tearoom
retard (être en)	to be late	saluer	to greet
retour, m	return	sang, m	blood
rêve, m	dream	sans	without
réveiller	to wake up	sans doute	doubtless
réveillé	awake	santé, f	health
revenir*	to return	satisfait	satisfied
rez-de- chaussée, m	ground floor	sauter	to jump
		sauvage	wild
rhume, m	cold	sauver	to save
riche	rich	savoir	to know
rien	nothing	savoir, m	knowledge
rire*	to laugh	savon, m	soap
rivière, f	stream	sec	dry
riz, m	rice	sécher	to dry
robe, f	dress	seconde, f	second
robinet, m	faucet, tap	secret	secret
rocher, m	rock	sécurité, f	security
roi, m	king		

124

séjour, m	stay	sommet, m	summit
sel	salt	son, m	sound
semaine, f	week	sonner	to sound
semblable	similar	sonnette, f	bell, buzzer
sembler	to seem	sorte, f	sort, kind
sens, m	sense	sortie, f	exit
sentiment, m	feeling	sortir*	to exit
sentir	to feel	souci, m	worry
séparer	to separate	soudain	suddenly
sérieux	serious	soupe, f	soup
serrure, f	lock	sourd	deaf
service, m	service	sous	under
serviette, f	towel	sous réserve	on condition
servir*	to serve	souvenir* de (se)	to remember
seul	alone		
seulement	only	souvent	often
sévère	severe	spécial	special
si	if	sport, m	sport
si !	of course!	station-service, f	service station
siècle, m	century		
signature, f	signature	stupide	stupid
signe, m	sign	succès, m	success
signer	to sign	sucre, m	sugar
signifier	to signify	sucré	sweet
s'il vous plaît	please	sud, m	south
silence, m	silence	suivre*	to follow
simple	simple	superflu	superfluous
situation, f	situation	supporter	to support, to tolerate
sœur, f	sister		
soif, f	thirsty	supposer	to suppose
soigneusement	carefully	sur	on, over, about
soin, m	care	sûr	sure, safe
soir, m	evening	sûrement	surely
sol, m	floor	surpris	surprised
soldes, m	sale	surtout	above all
soleil, m	sun		
sombre	shadow	**T**	
somme, f	sum		
sommeil, m	sleep	tabac, m	tobacco
		table, f	table

tache, f	stain
taille, f	size
taire* (se)	to shut up
tante, f	aunt
tard	late
tasse, f	cup
taxi, m	taxi
tel	such
téléphone, m	telephone
téléphoner	to telephone
télévision, f	television
témoin, m	witness
tempête, f	storm
temps, m	weather
temps (en même)	at the same time
tendre	tender
tenir*	to hold, to keep
tente, f	tent
terminer	to finish
terminus, m	terminal
terre, f	earth
tête, f	head
thé, m	tea
tiers, m	third
timbre, m	stamp
tirer	to shoot
tissu	cloth
toit, m	roof
tomber	to fall
tôt	early
toucher	to touch
toujours	always
tour, f	tower
tourner	to turn
tourner (à droite)	to turn right
tous	all
tous les deux	both

tout	all, everything
tout de suite	right away
tout droit	straight ahead
toxique	toxic
trace, f	track
traduire*	to translate
train, m	train
traitement, m	treatment
traiter	to treat
tranquille	calm
tranquillité	tranquility
transpirer	to perspire
travail, m	work
travailler	to work
travailleur/se	worker
travers (à)	across, through
traversée, f	crossing
très	very
triste	sad
tromper	to deceive
tromper (se)	to be wrong about
trop de (sing.)	too much
trop de (pl)	to many
trou, m	hole
trouver	to find
trouver (se)	to find oneself

U

unique	unique
université, f	university
urgent	urgent
usage, m	usage
usine, f	factory
utile	useful
utiliser	to use

V

vacances, f pl	vacation
vague, f	wave
vain (en)	in vain
valable	valid
valeur, f	value
valise, f	suitcase
vallée, f	valley
vapeur, m	steam
vendre	to sell
venir*	to come
vent, m	wind
vente, f	sale
verglas, m	frost
vérifier	to verify, to check
vérité, f	truth
verre, m	glass
vert	green
vêtements	clothes
viande, f	meat
vide	empty
vie, f	life
vieux, vielle	old
village, m	village
ville, f	city
virage, m	bend
vis, f	screw
visage, m	face
visible	visible
visite, f	visit
visiter	to visit
vite	fast
vitesse, f	speed
vitre, f	windowpane
vitrine, f	show window
vivant	alive
vivre*	to live
voie, f	lane, road, way
voile, f	sail
voir	to see
voisin, m	neighbor
voiture, f	car
voix, f	voice
vol, m	flight
voler	to steel
voleur, m	thief
volontiers	willingly
voter	to vote
vouloir*	to want
voyage, m	trip
voyager	to travel
vrai	real
vue, f	view

Z

zéro	zero

English-French

A

English	French
a long time	longtemps
a lot	beaucoup
abbreviation	abréviation, f
able	capable
abode	logis, m
about	à peu près, environ, autour de, sur
above	en haut
above all	surtout
absent	absent
absolutely	absolument
abuse	abus, m
accelerate, to	accélérer
accept, to	accepter
access	accès, m
accident	accident, m
accompany, to	accompagner
achieve, to	réaliser
acknowledge, to	reconnaître*
across	à travers
act, to	agir
activity	activité, f
addition	addition, f
address	adresse, f
administration	administration, f
admire, to	admirer
advantage	avantage, m
advertisement	annonce, f, publicité, f
afraid of, to be	craindre*
after	après
afternoon	après-midi, m or f
again	de nouveau
against	contre
age	âge, m
agency	agence, f
ago	il y a
agreed	D'accord !
air	air, m
airplane	avion, m
airport	aéroport, m
alive	vivant
all	tout, tous
allow, to	permettre*
almost	presque
alone	seul
already	déjà
also	aussi
although	bien que
altitude	altitude, f
always	toujours
ambassador	ambassadeur, m
among	parmi
amount	montant, m
and	et
anger	colère, f
animal	animal, m
annual	annuel
another	autre
answer	réponse, f
answer, to	répondre
any old way	n'importe quoi
anywhere	n'importe où
apartment	appartement, m
apparatus	appareil, m
apparently	apparemment
apple	pomme, f
appointment	redez-vous, m
appreciative	reconnaissant
approach, to	s'approcher

area	étendue, f	bank	banque, f / quai, m
arm	bras, m		
around	environ, autour de	bargain, to	marchander
		bath	bain, m
arrival	arrivée, f	bath, to	baigner (se)
arrive, to	arriver	bathing suit	maillot de bain, m
art	art, m		
article	article	bay	baie, f
artist	artiste, m + f	be, to	être*
as	comme	be able, to	être* capable de
as if	comme si	be cold, to	avoir* froid
at first	d'abord	be composed of, to	se composer de
at least	au moins		
ATM	distributeur automatique, m	be friends, to	être* ami(e)
		be hungry, to	avoir* faim
attempt	essai, m	be introduced, to	faire* la connaissance de
attempt, to	essayer		
attest, to	attester	be late, to	être* en retard
aunt	tante, f	be lying down, to	être* couché
authentic	authentique		
authorized to	autorisé (à)	be missing, to	manquer
automatic	automatique	be right, to	avoir* raison
autumn	automne, m	be seated, to	être* assis
average	moyen	be standing, to	être* debout
avoid, to	éviter	be thirsty, to	avoir* soif
awake	réveillé	be tired, to	être fatigué
		be wrong about, to	se tromper
B			
		be wrong, to	avoir* tort
baby	bébé, m	beach	plage, f
back	dos, m	beat, to	battre*
backpack	sac à dos, m	beauty	beauté, f
bad	mauvais	because	parce que
bad luck	malchance, f	become, to	devenir*
bag	sac, m	bed	lit, m
baker	boulanger, m	bee	abeille, f
bakery	boulangerie, f	beef	bœuf, m
ball	bal, m / ballon, m	beer	bière, f
		before	avant

before yesterday	avant-hier	bother, to	déranger / molester
begin, to	commencer	bottle	bouteille, f
beginning	début, m	bouquet	bouquet, m
behind	en arrière, derrière	box	boîte, f
		boy	garçon, m
Belgian	belge	bracelet	bracelet, m
Belgium	Belgique	brain	cerveau, m
believe, to	croire	branch	branche, f
bell	sonnette, f	bread	pain, m
below	au-dessous de, en bas	break	casser
		breakdown	panne
bench	banc, m	breakfast	petit déjeuner, m
bend	virage, m	breast	poitrine, f
berry	baie, f	breathe, to	respirer
best	meilleur	bridge	pont, m
between	entre	brother	frère, m
beyond	au-delà de	brother-in-law	beau-frère, m
bicycle	bicyclette, f	brunette	brune
big	grand / gros	brush	brosse, f
bird	oiseau, m	building	bâtiment, m
birth	naissance, f	bulb	ampoule, f
bitter	amer	bus	bus, m, car, m
black	noir	business	affaire, f
blanket	couverture, f	busy	occupé
bleed, to	saigner	but	mais
blind	aveugle	butter	beurre, m
blond	blond	button	bouton, m
blood	sang, m	buy, to	acheter
blow	coup, m	buzzer	sonnette, f
blue	bleu	by chance	par hasard
boat	bateau, m	by heart	par cœur
body	corps		
bone	os, m	**C**	
book	livre, m		
border	frontière, f	cabin	cabane, f
boring	ennuyeux	calculate	calculer
born	né	calendar	calendrier, m
borrow, to	emprunter	call, to	appeler
both	tous les deux		

call back, to	rappeler	circumstances	circonstances, f pl
call oneself, to	s'appeler		
calm	calme, tranquille	city	ville, f
camp site	camping, m	class	classe, f
candle	bougie, f	clean	propre
capital	capitale	clean, to	nettoyer
car	voiture, f	close, to	fermer
card	carte, f	closed	fermé
care	soin, m	cloth	tissu
carefully	soigneusement	clothes	vêtements
carry, to	porter	cloud	nuage, m
cash	espèces, f, liquide, m	coach	car, m
		coast	côte, f
castel	château, m	coat	manteau, m
cat	chat, m	cock	coq
catch, to	attraper	coffee	café, m
cathedral	cathédrale, f	coffee shop	café, m
cause	cause, f	coins	monnaie, f
cause, to	causer	cold	froid / rhume, m
cellar	cave, f	collect, to	collectionner
cemetery	cimetière, m	color	couleur, f
center	centre, m	comb	peigne, m
century	siècle, m	come in!	entrez !
certain	certain	come, to	venir*
chair	chaise, f	comfortable	confortable
change	change, m	company	entreprise, f
change, to	changer	compare, to	comparer
charge, to	charger	comparison	comparaison, f
check	chèque, m	complain	plainte, f
check, to	vérifier	complain, to	se plaindre*
cheerful	gai	complete, to	achever / remplir
cheese	fromage, m		
child	enfant, m + f	completely	complètement
choice	choix, m	concerning	concernant
chose, to	choisir	condition	condition, f
Christmas	Noël	confidence	confiance
church	église, f	confirm, to	confirmer
cinema	cinéma, m	confuse, to	confondre
circulation	circulation, f	congratulations	félicitations, f pl

consent, to	consentir*
considerable	considérable
construct, to	construire*
consume, to	consommer
content	content
contents	contenu, m
contest	concours, m
continue, to	continuer
contract	contrat, m
conversation	conversation, f
convince, to	convaincre*
cook, to	faire* la cuisine
cooked	cuit
cord	corde
corner	coin, m
correspondence	correspondance
cost	frais, m
cost, to	coûter
costly	coûteux
cotton	coton, m
count, to	compter
country	pays, m
court	cour, f
crazy	fou
crime	crime, m
crossing	traversée, f
cry, to	pleurer
cup	tasse, f
cupboard	armoire, f
curious	curieux
current	courant, m
custom	coutume, f
customs	douane, f
cut, to	couper

D

daily	quotidien
damage	dommage, m

damp	humide
dance	danse, f
dance, to	danser
danger	danger, m
dangerous	dangereux
dare, to	oser
darkness	obscurité, f
date	date, f
daughter	fille, f
day	jour, m
day-off	congé, m
daytime	le jour
dead	mort
deaf	sourd
deal with, to	s'occuper de
dear	cher
death	mort, f
deceive, to	tromper
decide, to	décider
decision	décision, f
declare, to	déclarer
deep	profond
defend, to	défendre
deliberately	expressément
deliver, to	livrer
dentist	dentiste, m
deny, to	nier
department store	grand magasin, m
departure	départ, m
deposit	consigne, f
desire	désir, m
desire, to	désirer
desk	bureau, m
despite	malgré
destroy, to	détruire*
detail	détail, m
detour	détour, m
develop, to	développer

development	développement, m	drink	boisson, f
		drink, to	boire*
deviation	déviation, f	drinkable	potable
die, to	mourir*	drive, to	conduire
difference	différence, f	driver	chauffer
different	différent	drop	goutte, f
difficult	difficile	dry	sec
difficulty	difficulté, f	dry, to	sécher
dine, to	dîner	duration	durée, f
direct	direct	during	pendant
direction	direction, f	dust	poussière, f
directory	annuaire, m		
dirt	saleté, f	**E**	
dirty	sale		
disagreeable	désagréable	each person	chacun
disappear, to	disparaître*	each time	chaque fois
disappointed	déçu	ear	oreille, f
discharge, to	décharger	earlier	plus tôt
discover, to	découvrir*	early	tôt
disk	disque, m	earth	terre, f
disorder	désordre, m	east	est, m
dispute	dispute, f	Easter	Pâques
distinguish, to	distinguer	easy	facile
distrust	méfiance, f	eat, to	manger
dive, to	plonger	edible	comestible
divide, to	diviser	education	éducation, f
divide up, to	répartir	effect	effet, m
do, to	faire*	efficient	efficace
doctor	médecin, m	effort	effort, m
dog	chien, m	egg	œuf, m
door	porte, f	either... or	ou... ou
double	double	elections	élections, f
doubt	doute, m	elevator	ascenseur, m
doubtless	sans doute	elsewhere	ailleurs
down	bas	emergency	cas d'urgence, m
dozen	douzaine, f		
draw, to	dessiner	employ, to	employer
dream	rêve, m	employee	employé, m, employée, f
dress	robe, f		

empty	vide	extent	étendue, f
end	fin	external	externe
enough	assez	extraordinary	extraordinaire
enter, to	entrer	eye	œil, m
entry	entrée, f		
envelop	enveloppe, f	**F**	
environment	environne-ment, m		
		fabric	étoffe, f
equal	égal	face	visage, m
error	erreur, f	fact	fait, m
estimate, to	estimer	factory	usine, f
even	même	fake	faux
evening	soir, m	fall	automne, m
event	événement, m	fall, to	tomber
everyday	tous les jours	fall asleep, to	s'endormir
everywhere	partout	family	famille, f
exact	exact	famous	célèbre
exactly	justement	far	loin
exaggerated	exagéré	farm	ferme, f
examine, to	examiner	farmer	paysan, m
example	exemple, m	far-off	éloigné
excellent	excellent	fast	rapide, vite
exception	exception, f	fat	gros, gras
exchange	échange, m	father	père, m
exchange, to	échanger	faucet	robinet, m
excursion	excursion, f	fault	défaut, m, faute, f
excuse me	pardon !		
excuse, to	excuser, pardonner	fear	peur, f, crainte, f
		feeble	faible
exercise, to	exercer	feel, to	sentir
exhibition	exposition, f	feeling	sentiment, m
exit	sortie, f	feminine	féminin
exit, to	sortir*	fever	fièvre, f
expenses	dépenses, f	field	champ, m
expensive	cher	figure	chiffre, m
experience	expérience, f	fill, to	remplir
expired	périmé	finally	enfin, finalement
explain, to	expliquer		
expression	expression, f	find, to	trouver

find oneself, to	se trouver
finger	doigt, m
finish, to	terminer
fire	feu, m, incendie, m
firm	entreprise, f
first name	prénom, m
fish	poisson, m
fish, to	pêcher
fisherman	pêcheur, m
fix, to	fixer
flamenco	flamenco
flammable	inflammable
flash	éclair, m
flashlight	lampe de poche, f
flat	plat
flight	vol, m
floor	plancher, m / sol, m
flow, to	couler
flower	fleur, f
flower, to	fleurir*
fly	mouche, f
fog	brouillard, m
follow, to	suivre*
food	nourriture, f
foot	pied, m
for	pour
forbidden	interdit
force	force, f
force, to	forcer
foreigner	étranger, m / étranger/e
forest	forêt, f
forget, to	oublier
fork	fourchette, f
form	fiche, f
formerly	autrefois

fragile	fragile
France	France, f
free	libre / gratuit
French	Français / français/e
fresh	frais
friend	ami/e
friendly	aimable
frightful	affreux
from	de
from where	d'où
frost	verglas, m
fruit	fruit, m
full	plein
function, to	fonctionner
functioning	fonctionnement
furious	furieux
furniture	meuble, m
future	avenir, m / futur

G

garbage	ordures, f pl
garden	jardin, m
garlic	ail, m
gasoline	essence, f
gate	grille, f
general	général
get angry, to	se fâcher
get dressed, to	s'habiller
get married, to	se marier
get up, to	se lever
get used to, to	s'habituer
gift	cadeau, m
girl	fille, f
give for free, to	offrir*
give, to	donner
glass	verre, m

glasses	lunettes, f	happy	heureux
go, to	aller*	hard	dur
go down, to	descendre	hare	lièvre, m
go get, to	aller* chercher	harmful	nuisible
go shopping, to	faire* des courses	have, to	avoir*
		have fun, to	s'amuser
go up, to	monter	head	tête, f
goal	but, m	head (for), to	se diriger
good	bon	health	santé, f
government	gouverne-ment, m	hear, to	entendre
		heart	cœur, m
granddaughter	petite-fille, f	heat	chaleur, f
grandfather	grand-père, m	heating	chauffage, m
grandmother	grand-mère, f	heavy	poids, m / lourd
grandson	petit-fils, m	help someone, to	aider qqn
grape	raisin, m		
grasp, to	saisir	here	ici, là
grave	grave	hesitate, to	hésiter
green	vert	hike	randonnée, f
greet, to	saluer	hill	colline, f
grey	gris	history	histoire, f
ground floor	rez-de-chaussée, m	hold, to	tenir*
		hole	trou, m
group	groupe, m	holiday	jour de fête, m
grow, to	pousser	homework	devoir, m
guide	guide, m	honey	miel, m
guide, to	guider	hope, to	espérer
		horrible	horrible
H		horse	cheval, m
		hospital	hôpital, m
habit	habitude, f	hot	chaud
hair	cheveux, m	hotel	hôtel, m
hairdresser	coiffeur, m	hour	heure, f
half	moitié, f / demi	hourly	à l'heure
hall	salle, f	house	maison, f
hammer	marteau, m	how	comment
hand	main, f	how much?	combien ?
handkerchief	mouchoir, m	hunger	faim, f
handsome	beau	hungry, to be	avoir faim

hurry, to	se dépêcher	inspector	contrôleur, m
husband	mari, m	instead of	au lieu de
		insufficient	insuffisant
I		insurance	assurance, f
		insure, to	assurer
ice cream	glace, f	intelligent	intelligent
idea	idée, f	intend, to	avoir*
identity card	carte		l'intention
	d'identité, f	intention	intention, f
if	si	interesting	intéressant
ignite, to ·	allumer	interpreter	interprète, m + f
illness	maladie, f	interrupt, to	interrompre
important	important	intersection	carrefour, m
impossible	impossible	intolerable	insupportable
imprecise	imprécis	invent, to	inventer
impression	impression, f	invitation	invitation, f
improve, to	améliorer	invite, to	inviter
imprudent	imprudent	island	île, f
in	dans, en	itinerary	itinéraire, m
in front	devant		
in front of	en face de	**J**	
in the midst of	au milieu de		
increase, to	augmenter	jam	confiture, f
incredible	incroyable	jewelry	bijou, m
indecent	indécent	joke	blague, f,
indispensable	indispensable		plaisanterie, f
inevitable	inévitable	joy	joie, f
inexpensive	pas cher	judge, to	juger
inform	se renseigner	juice	jus, m
oneself, to		jump, to	sauter
information	information, f,	just	juste
	renseignement,		
	m	**K**	
inhabit, to	habiter		
inhabitant	habitant, m	keep, to	tenir* / garder
inn	auberge, f	key	clé, f
innocent	innocent	king	roi, m
inside	à l'intérieur	kiss	baiser, m
insist upon, to	insister sur	kiss, to	embrasser
insolent	insolent	kitchen	cuisine, f

knee	genou, m	liberty	liberté, f
knife	couteau, m	license	permis
knocked over	renversé	lie	mensonge, m
know, to	savoir	life	vie, f
know, to (person or place)	connaître*	light	lumière, f / clair, léger
knowledge	savoir, m, connaissance, f	light up, to	éclairer
		lighter	briquet, m
known	connu	like	comme
		like that	comme ça
L		like, to	aimer bien
		line	ligne, f
lack of	manque (de), m	lip	lèvre, f
lack, to	manquer	liquid	liquide
lake	lac, m	list	liste, f
landscape	paysage, m	listen, to	écouter
lane	ruelle, f, voie, f	lit up	illuminé
language	langue, f	liter	litre, m
last	dernier, m, dernière, f	little	peu
		live, to	vivre*
last, to	durer	liver	foie, m
late	tard	lock	serrure, f
later	après, plus tard	lock, to	fermer (à clé)
laugh, to	rire*	long	long
law	loi, f, droit, m	look	regard, m
laziness	paresseux	look at, to	regarder
leaf	feuille, f	lose, to	perdre
learn, to	apprendre	love, to	aimer
leather	cuir, m	loved one	amour, m
leave, to	partir*, laisser, quitter	luck	chance, f
		luggage	bagages, m
left, on the	à gauche	lunch, to have	déjeuner, m
left-overs	reste, m		
leisure	loisirs, m	**M**	
lend, to	prêter		
length	longueur, f	machine	appareil, m, machine, f
lengthen, to	allonger	mailbox	boîte aux lettres, f
let, to	laisser		
letter	lettre, f		

mailman (woman)	facteur, m	modern	moderne
make, to	faire*	modify, to	modifier
make an effort, to	faire* un effort	molest, to	molester
		moment	moment, m
make love, to	faire* l'amour	money	argent, m, monnaie, f
make possible, to	rendre possible	month	mois, m
malicious	malicieux	monthly	mensuel, par mois
man	homme, m		
manner	manière, f	monument	monument, m
map	carte géographique, f	moon	lune, f
		more	encore, plus
		more like	plutôt
market	marché, m	more or less	plus ou moins
masculine	masculin	morning	matin
match	allumette, f	mosquito	moustique, m
maybe	peut-être	mother	mère, f
meal	repas, m	motor	moteur, m
means	moyen	motorcycle	moto, f
measure	mesure, f	mountain	montagne, f
measure, to	mesurer	mouth	bouche, f
meat	viande, f	move out, to	déménager
Mediterranean	Méditerranée, f	movement	mouvement, m
meet, to	rencontrer	movie camera	caméra, f
menu	carte, f	Mrs.	madame
merchandise	marchandise, f	mud	boue, f
meter	mètre, m	museum	musée, m
middle	milieu, m	mushroom	champignon, m
midnight	minuit	music	musique, f
mild	doux	must	devoir*
milk	lait, m	moustache	moustache, f
minute	minute, f		
mirror	miroir, m	**N**	
miserly	avare		
misfortune	malheur, m	nail	clou, m
Miss	mademoiselle	name	nom, m
mister	monsieur	narrow	étroit
misunderstanding	malentendu, m	nasty	méchant
		nation	nation, f

nationality	nationalité, f
natural	naturel
nature	nature, f
near	proche
necessary	nécessaire
neck	cou, m
need	besoin, m
need, to	avoir* besoin de
neglect, to	négliger
neighbor	voisin, m
neighborhood	quartier, m
neither... nor	ni... ni
nephew	neveu, m
net	filet, m
never	jamais
new	nouveau
news	nouvelle, f
newspaper	journal, m
next	prochain, m, prochaine, f
next	ensuite
next to	à côté de
nice	beau, agréable, gentil
niece	nièce, f
night	nuit, f
nightclub	boîte de nuit, f
nine	neuf
no	non
no one	personne, f
nobody	personne
noise	bruit, m
noisy	bruyant
none	aucun
noon	midi, m
normal	normal
north	nord, m
nose	nez, m
not	pas

not even	même pas
not yet	pas encore
note	note, f
notebook	cahier, m
nothing	rien
notice, to	remarquer
notify, to	prévenir* qqn
now	maintenant
nowhere	nulle part
nude	nu
number	chiffre, m, nombre, m, numéro, m
numerous	nombreux

O

object	objet, m
observe, to	observer
obstruct, to	empêcher
occasion	occasion, f
occupied	occupé
ocean	océan, m
of	de
of course	bien sûr
offend, to	offenser
offer	offre, f
office	bureau, m
often	souvent
oil	huile, f
okay	d'accord !
old	vieux
on	en, sur
on condition	sous réserve
on foot	à pied
on time	à l'heure
once	une fois
only	seulement
open	ouvert

open, to	ouvrir*	patience	patience, f
opera	opéra, m	pay a visit, to	rendre visite
opinion	opinion, f	pay attention, to	faire* attention à
opposed	opposé		
opposite	contraire, m	pay in cash, to	payer en espèces
or	ou	pay, to	payer, régler
order	commande, f / ordre, m	peace	paix, f
		pear	poire, f
order, to	commander	pencil	crayon, m
other	autre	people	gens, m pl, peuple, m
otherwise	autrement		
out of stock	épuisé	pepper	poivre, m
out of the question	hors de question	percent	pour-cent, m
		perfect	parfait
outside	dehors	permanent	permanent
outside, on the	à l'extérieur	permission	permission, f
over	sur	permit, to	permettre*
owner	propriétaire, m, patron, m	person	personne
		personal	personnel
		perspire (to)	transpirer
P		persuade, to	persuader
		pharmacy	pharmacie, f
package	paquet, m	phone call	coup de téléphone, m
page	page, f		
pain	douleur, f	photo	photo, f
paint, to	peindre*	pickpocket	pickpocket, m
painting	peinture, f	piece	morceau, m, pièce, f
pale	pâle		
pan	poêle, m	pig	porc, m
pants	pantalon, m	pill	pilule, f
paper	papier, m	pillowcase	oreiller, m
pardon!	pardon !	pimple	bouton, m
parent	parent	pin	épingle, f
parents	parents, m pl	pity!	dommage !
park	parc, m	place	endroit, m, lieu, m, place, f
park, to	se garer		
parking	parking, m	place, to	mettre*
passport	passeport, m	plan	plan, m
past	passé	plant	plante, f
path	chemin, m	plate	assiette, f

play	jeu, m	product	produit, m
play, to	jouer	profession	profession, f
playing cards	jeu de cartes, m	professor	professeur, m
please	s'il vous plaît,	progress	progrès, m
	s'il te plaît	promise, to	promettre*
please, to	plaire*	pronounce, to	prononcer
pleasure	plaisir, m	pronunciation	prononciation, f
plus	plus	proof	preuve, f
pocket	poche, f	propose, to	proposer
police	police, f	proposition	proposition, f
police officer	agent de	proprietor	patron, m
	police, m	prospectus	prospectus, m
pond	étang, m	protection	protection, f
poor	pauvre	protest, to	protester
port	port, m	prove, to	prouver
possess, to	posséder	provide, to	procurer, fournir
possible	possible	prudent	prudent
post office	poste, f	public	public
postcard	carte postale, f	pupil	élève, m + f
pot	casserole, f	purchase	achat, m
potato	pomme de	pure	pur
	terre, f	purpose (on)	exprès
powder	poudre, f	put together, to	ressembler
power	pouvoir*	put, to	mettre*
practical	pratique		
precaution	précaution, f	**Q**	
prefer, to	préférer		
pregnant	enceinte	quality	qualité, f
prepare, to	préparer	quantity	quantité, f
present	présent	quarter	quart, m
present, to	présenter	queen	reine, f
pretext	prétexte, m	question	question, f
pretty	joli	quit, to	quitter
prevent, to	prévenir* qqn,		
	empêcher	**R**	
price	prix, m		
prison	prison, f	radio	radio, f
private	privé	rain	pluie, f
probable	probable	rain, to	pleuvoir*
procure, to	procurer	rare	rare

143

rather	plutôt	respect, to	respecter
ravishing	ravissant	responsible	responsable
raw	cru	rest	repos, m
razor	rasoir, m	rest, to	se reposer
read, to	lire*	restaurant	bistrot, m
ready	prêt	result	résultat, m
real	réel, vrai	return	retour, m
reality	réalité, f	return, to	revenir*
reason	raison, f	rib	côte, f
reasonable	raisonnable	rice	riz, m
receive, to	recevoir*	rich	riche
recently	récemment	right	droit
reception	réception, f	right (to be)	avoir raison
recommend, to	recommander	right away	tout de suite
record	disque, m	right, to the	à droite
red	rouge	rights	droits, m
reduction	réduction, f	ring	bague, f
refrigerator	frigidaire, m	ripe	mûr
refuse, to	refuser	river	fleuve, m
region	région, f	road	voie, f
regret	regret, m	rock	rocher, m
regret, to	regretter	roof	toit, m
reimburse, to	rembourser	room	chambre, f,
relax, to	se reposer		salle, f
remaining	restant		
remains	restes, m pl	rooster	coq
remember, to	se souvenir* de	rotten	pourri
render, to	rendre	round	rond
rendez-vous	rendez-vous, m	run, to	courir*
rent	loyer, m	rushed	pressé
rent, to	louer		
reparation	réparation, f	**S**	
repeat, to	répéter		
replace, to	remplacer	sack	sac, m
representation	représentation, f	sad	triste
request	demande, f	safe	sûr
request, to	demander	sail	voile, f
reserve	réserve	salad	salade, f
reserve, to	réserver	sale	vente, f /
resolve, to	résoudre*		soldes, m
		salt	sel

salty	salé	shirt	chemise, f
same	pareil	shoemaker	cordonnier
same, the	le même	shoe	chaussure, f
sand	sable, m	shoot, to	tirer
satisfied	satisfait	short	court
save, to	sauver / épargner	shortage	manque, m
		short cut	raccourci, m
say, to	dire*	shortly	prochainement
scale	balance, f	shoulder	épaule, f
school	école, f	shout, to	crier
scissors	ciseaux, m	show	émission, f
screw	vis, f	show window	vitrine, f
sea	mer, f	show, to	montrer
search, to	chercher	shower	douche, f
season	saison	shut up, to	se taire*
second	deuxième / seconde, f	sick, ill	malade
		side	côté, f
secret	secret	sign	signe, m
security	sécurité, f	sign, to	signer
see, to	voir	signature	signature, f
seem, to	avoir* l'air, sembler	signify, to	signifier
		silence	silence, m
seize, to	saisir	similar	semblable
sell, to	vendre	simple	simple
send, to	envoyer	since	depuis
sense	sens, m	since, as	puisque
sentence	phrase, f	sing, to	chanter
separate, to	séparer	single	célibataire
serious	sérieux, grave	sister	sœur, f
serve, to	servir*	sister-in-law	belle-sœur, f
service	service, m	sit (oneself)	
service station	station-service, f	down, to	s'asseoir*
severe	sévère	situation	situation, f
sew, to	coudre*	size	taille, f
shadow	ombre, f	skin	peau, f
share, to	partager	skinny	maigre
sharp	aigu	skirt	jupe, f
sheet	feuille, f / drap, m	sky	ciel, m
		skyscraper	gratte-ciel, m
shine, to	briller		

sleep	sommeil, m	stain	tache, f
sleep, to	dormir*	staircase	escalier, m
sleeping bag	sac de couchage, m	stamp	timbre, m
		star	étoile, f
slim	mince	state	État, m
slow	lent	statement	déclaration, f
smell	odeur, f	station	gare, f
smoke, to	fumer	stay	séjour, m
smoke	fumée, f	stay, to	rester
snail	escargot, m	steam	vapeur, m
snow	neige, f	steel, to	voler
soap	savon, m	stick	bâton, m
sock	chaussette, f	stink, to	puer
soft	mou, doux	still	encore
some	quelques, pl	sting, to	piquer
somebody	quelqu'un	stomach	estomac, m
someone	quelqu'un	stone	pierre, f
something	quelque chose	stop	arrêt, m
sometimes	parfois	stop, to	arrêter
son	fils, m	store	magasin, m
song	chanson, f	storm	orage, m, tempête, f
soon	bientôt		
sorry, to be	être* désolé	story	histoire, f
sort	sorte, f	straight ahead	tout droit
sound	son, m	strange	bizarre, étrange
sound, to	sonner	stream	rivière, f
soup	soupe, f	street	rue, f
sour	acide	strength	force, f
south	sud, m	stroke	coup, m
space	espace, m	strike, to	frapper
speak, to	parler	stroll, to	se promener
special	spécial	strong	fort
speed	vitesse, f	student	étudiant/e
spell, to	épeler	study, to	faire* des études
spend, to	dépenser		
spirit	esprit, m	stupid	bête, stupide
spoon	cuillère, f	suburbs	banlieue, f
sport	sport, m	success	succès, m
spring	printemps, m	such	tel
square	carré	suddenly	soudain

sugar	sucre, m	terminal	terminus, m
suitcase	valise	thank you	merci
sum	somme, f	thank, to	remercier
summer	été, m	thanks to	grâce à
summit	sommet, m	that	que
sun	soleil, m	the day after	
superfluous	superflu	tomorrow	après-demain
support, to	supporter	then	ensuite
suppose, to	supposer	there	là-bas
sure	sûr	there is / are	il y a
surely	sûrement	therefore	donc
surprise	surprise	thick	épais
surroundings	environs, m	thief	voleur, m
sweet	doux, sucré	thing	chose, f
swim, to	se baigner, nager	think, to	penser
swimming pool	piscine, f	third	tiers, m
		thirsty	soif, f
		thread	fil, m
T		throat	gorge, f
		through	à travers
table	table, f	throw, to	jeter
tablet	comprimé, m	ticket	billet, m
take, to	prendre*	time, at the	à cette époque
talk, to	parler	time, at the	
tan, to	bronzer	same	en même temps
task	devoir, m	tip	pourboire, m
taste	goût, m	tire	pneu, m
taxi	taxi, m	tired	fatigué
tea	thé, m	tiring	fatigant
tearoom	salon de thé, m	to	à
teach, to	enseigner	tobacco	tabac, m
teacher	professeur, m	today	aujourd'hui
telephone	téléphone, m	together	ensemble
telephone, to	téléphoner	tolerate, to	supporter
television	télévision, f	tomorrow	demain
tell, to	dire*, raconter	too many	trop (pl)
temporarily	provisoirement	too much	trop de
tend to, to	s'occuper de	tool	outil, m
tender	tendre	tooth	dent, f
tent	tente, f		

torch	lampe de poche, f
touch, to	toucher
tow, to	remorquer
towel	serviette, f
tower	tour, f
toxic	toxique
track	trace, f
train	train, m
tranquility	tranquillité
translate, to	traduire*
trap, to	attraper
travel, to	voyager
treat, to	traiter
treatment	traitement, m
tree	arbre, m
trip	voyage, m
truck	camion, m
truth	vérité, f
turn off, to	éteindre*
turn right, to	tourner (à droite)
turn, to	tourner
twilight	crépuscule, m

U

ugly	laid
umbrella	parapluie, m
uncertain	incertain
uncle	oncle, m
under	sous
understand, to	comprendre*
undress, to	se déshabiller
uneasy	mal à l'aise
unexpected	inattendu
unfortunately	malheureusement
unique	unique
university	université, f

unjust	injuste
unknown	inconnu
unload, to	décharger
until	jusqu'à
up	haut
up to here	jusqu'ici
urgent	urgent
usage	usage, m
use, to	utiliser
useful	utile
useless	inutile
usual	habituel

V

vacation	vacances, f
vain (in)	en vain
valid	valable
valley	vallée, f
value	valeur, f
vegetables	légumes, m
verify, to	vérifier
very	très
view	vue, f
village	village, m
visible	visible
visit	visite, f
visit, to	visiter
voice	voix, f
vote, to	voter

W

wait, to	attendre
wake up, to	réveiller
walk, to	marcher
wall	mur, m
wallet	portefeuille, m
want, to	vouloir*
war	guerre, f

warn, to	avertir, prévenir	winter	hiver, m
wash yourself,		wire	fil, m
to	se laver	with	avec
wash, to	laver	within	dedans
watch	montre, f	without	sans
watch out!	attention !, f	witness	témoin, m
watch over, to	garder	woman	femme, f
watchful	attentif	wood	bois, m
water	eau, f	wool	laine, f
wave	vague, f	word	mot, m
way	chemin, m,	work	œuvre, f,
	voie, f /		travail, m
	manière, f	work, to	travailler
we	on	worker	ouvrier, m,
weak	faible		travailleur/se
weakness	faiblesse, f	world	monde, m
weather	temps, m	worn out	épuisé
wedding	mariage, m	worry	souci, m
week	semaine, f	worry, to	s'inquiéter
weekly	hebdomadaire	wound	blessure, f
weigh, to	peser	write, to	écrire*
welcome	bienvenue	writing	écriture, f
well	puits, m	writing paper	papier à lettre, m
west	ouest, m	wrong	faux
wet	mouillé, humide		
what?	quoi ?	**Y**	
wheel	roue, f		
when	quand	year	an, m, année, f
where	où	yellow	jaune
white	blanc	yes	oui
who	qui	yesterday	hier
whole	entier	young	jeune
why?	pourquoi ?		
wide	large	**Z**	
wild	sauvage		
willingly	volontiers	zero	zéro
win, to	gagner		
wind	vent, m		
window	fenêtre, f		
windowpane	vitre, f		

N° édition 1443: Guide FRENCH FROM THE WORD GO !

Achevé d'imprimer en juin 1998
sur les presses de l'Imprimerie De Beurs à Anvers.